Organizational Technocratic Work and Personality

Organizational Technocratic Work and Personality

An Actual Pure-Type

Robert-Theophilus Dauphin

Copyright © 2014 by Robert-Theophilus Dauphin.

Library of Congress Control Number: 2014915307
ISBN: Hardcover   978-1-4990-6526-8
       Softcover   978-1-4990-6528-2
       eBook   978-1-4990-6527-5

All rights reserved. No part of this book may be reproduced or transmitted in any form or by any means, electronic or mechanical, including photocopying, recording, or by any information storage and retrieval system, without permission in writing from the copyright owner.

Any people depicted in stock imagery provided by Thinkstock are models, and such images are being used for illustrative purposes only. Certain stock imagery © Thinkstock.

This book was printed in the United States of America.

Rev. date: 08/21/2014

To order additional copies of this book, contact:
Xlibris LLC
1-888-795-4274
www.Xlibris.com
Orders@Xlibris.com
663010

Contents

Chapter 1
Conceptual and Theoretical Foundation of Technocratic Personality 9
    Theoretical Description of Vital Expressions 13

Chapter 2
An Antiquated Perception of Personality and Work 14
    Official Classifications 14
    Cultural Differences 15
    Pure-Types 15

Chapter 3
Technocrat: a Pure-Type 18
    Current Professional Recognition 18
    Connection to Modernism 19
    Growth in Technocrats' Occupations 20
    The Technocratization of Work 20
    The First Path Is Demographic 21
    Contravening Professional Categories 22
    Technocrats' Work Is More Respectful of Existing Pure-Types 22

Chapter 4
Theoretical Perspectives on Technocratic Work and Governing 26
    Theoretical Perspectives on Technocratic Operational Process 27
        Recording Where a Technocrat's Time Goes 27
        Focusing Attention on Contributions 28
        Making Ability Productive 28
        Operating in Stages 28
        Making Productive Decisions 28

Chapter 5
Technocrats Are Experts 30
    Perspectives on the Conceptual Need for Technocrats 31

Conceptual Identification of Technocrats...................................33
Perspectives on Technocrat Realities 37
Perspective on Technocratic Productivity 42
Perspective on Technocratic Specialization....................................43

Chapter 6
Technocrats' Time and Task Identification............................. 47
Perspectives on Technocrats Operational-Time and Constraints... 48
Perspectives on Technocrats' Operational-Time Identification ... 52

Chapter 7
Perspectives on Limiting Unproductive Functions................................. 58
Perspectives on Merging Technocrats Optional
Operational-Time..62

Chapter 8
Technocratic Challenge.. 66
Specialized or Competent 66
Motivation to Perform Productively................................66
Promote Innovative Ideas 67
Enable Organizations to Act..68
Reassure Organizations of Productivity..........................68

Chapter 9
Perspectives on Technocratic Qualities and Characteristics 70
Persuasion...70
Collaborative Trait..71
Realism 71
Contributive Relationship 71
Developing Worth..71
Enhancement of Products/Services 71
Flexibility...71
Methodical Approach..72
Troubleshooting Skills 72
Facilitative Quality 72
Microtechnocratic Traits...72
Personal Traits 73
Operational Traits...74
Persuasive Traits...75
Collaborative Traits 75

Chapter 10
Operational Differences between Technocratic Work and Governing ... 77
    Enhancing Worth vs. Enhancing Motivation..............................77
    Circles of Success vs. Circles of Authority..................................77
    Operational Responsibility vs. Administrative Responsibility ...77
  The Big Picture...79

CHAPTER 1

Conceptual and Theoretical Foundation of Technocratic Personality

Books on technocratic personality and work have never been done. Conversely, books on leadership personality traits and work have increased over the years as leadership models have broadened and more fully incorporated a complete range of leadership attributes. Most technocratic attributes have not been influenced and have not been viewed in terms of the historic perspective of leadership behaviors, which is defined as either "initiating structure," which involve control of processes, task development, and workflow organization, or "consideration," which involve the development of emotional relationships. Thus, no self-described complete technocratic model has been established to challenge leadership perspectives that can define attributes that fall into various technocratic categories. Hence, I have learned that technocratic work is about mobilizing resources to perform productively and transforming organizations' resources into accomplishments, specializations into practicalities, ingenuities and unproductivity into productivity, and imagination into opportunities. Technocratic work is about creating an environment in which individuals turn challenges into productivity.

Throughout my professional life, I have never observed the scarcity of challenges within organizations. Although organizational challenges appear to be intensifying, nonetheless, some technocrats have transformed their organizations through persistence and operational expertise. These successes have not contributed in enhancing the way organizational technocrats are perceived and rewarded.

This is because institutions of higher learning and organizations have been preoccupied studying leadership personality traits and functions. They have neglected to conceptualize any other form of organizational personality traits that involve organizational operations and collaboration with leadership responsibilities and professional arrangements within organizations. Consequently, organizations have collapsed due to misidentification of certain individuals' characteristics. The United States (U.S.) healthcare industry is estimated to lose roughly five hundred thousand practitioners by 2025, partly because incompetent and defective leadership is an "epidemic" in every stage of health administration (Journal of Nursing, 2013).

Hogan (2008) suggests that bad leadership is the solitary, uttermost, and unrelenting problem in health administration. He says that over 65 percent of leaders within health administration organizations are inept, sub-substandard, or severely flawed, and a greater percentage exists within governmental organizations. Hogan writes that 50 percent to 75 percent of leaders in the United States are inept, and their ineptitude contributes fundamentally to employee discontent, turnover, and unproductivity.

Consequently, this theoretical observational analysis intends to establish the foundation for a new paradigm of organizational personality and relations of operations that reflect collaboration in the separation of responsibilities and professional arrangements of modernized organizations. It reveals the importance of the duties, responsibilities, and functions of "technocratic personality" (technocrats), an ever-existing organizational personality that has been overlooked for "leadership personality," an essential and more glamorous personality that has been well researched and extensively written about. This analytical perspective draws on sets of observational phenomena to propose an experiential foundation of organizational technocratic duties, responsibilities, functions, and traits.

Evidence that the nature of work within organizations is unstable is indisputable. Technocrats' work and contributions within organizations have been undervalued while those of leaders have been overvalued. Scholarship on various aspects of leadership by far exceeds scholarship on technocratic personality, if any at all exist. Administrative, managerial, and technical scholarships have become increasingly differentiated. Administrative and managerial education that focuses predominantly on leadership aspects of organization and management has constantly increased. Organizations search for and recruit individuals that they perceive possess leadership traits and potentials, even among individuals with technocratic personalities.

Most of the perspectives in this book of the traits, behaviors, and the differences of technocrats and leaders were personally and directly gleaned, and some are already established leadership and managerial perspectives that are used as a framework to explain technocratic personality traits. I observed colleagues that I worked with within the United States military and within the federal government. The theoretical concepts of this book seek to establish a framework about technocratic traits that are not abstract but grounded on and ingrained in my memory.

Thus, this theoretical framework involves a complicated, dynamic, repetitive process in which the establishment of the theory and the gleaning of the information build on one another. It involves a single exploratory form, which is generative in nature and helps with observations, gleaning, and the analytical process. Thus, the guide questions are not limited or confined solely to this analysis. What are the personality traits of technocrats? How are they different from people with leadership personality? These questions are tentative linkages between the core of the analysis and my observations.

Hence, technology has eradicated some forms of technocratic work, creating others and altering a huge segment of what remains. The segment that remains requires postsecondary education, demanding that organizations expand their operations significantly over the years. This upward trend toward postsecondary education is expected to continue. Competition among organizations has created this increased demand for a more educated workforce. This competition has created an additional burden on organizations to function within an ever-increasing competitive specialized environment and strive to recruit a specialized workforce and retain existing ones. The ability of organizations to determine the relationship between technocratic and leadership characteristics and organizational outcomes such as job satisfaction could provide the basis for developing training programs, which organizations can then use to obtain competitive advantage.

In addition to an increasingly competitive organizational environment, leaders are also confronted with a potential shortfall of specialized workforce. The first of the baby boomers (born between 1946 and 1964) that are currently working in technocratic or specialized positions are now eligible for social security, and the overall demographics of those over 65 within the United States is expected to increase from 12.4 percent in 2000 to 19.6 percent in 2030 (Government Accountability Office [GAO], 2006). Thus, an organizational awareness of technocratic personality will allow for the development of both current and future technocrats as organizations seek to obtain competitive advantage within the job market.

Growth and competitive expectations require increased accountability of organizational technocrats and leaders. Technocrats and leaders must become more aware of and accountable for increased organizational productivity and effectiveness. By identifying technocratic and leadership personalities that link to increased output and job satisfaction, individuals responsible for productivity and effectiveness can ensure that successful technocratic and leadership development programs are implemented and managed to maximize organizations' productivity and effectiveness. This improvement would have a direct relationship to organizations obtaining operational and competitive advantages.

Within any competitive organizational environment, technocrats and leaders must direct their focus on their impact on their organization's overall productivity and effectiveness. This analytical observational perspective addresses the technocratic personality trait and the impact that technocrats have on various components of organizations' productivity and effectiveness, i.e., output, job satisfaction, and more.

Technocrats and leaders are vital components within organizations; however, it is during times of potential emergency and transformation that the work of technocrats and leaders become of paramount importance. The very future of any organization usually depends on how expertly the individuals within the organization handle the challenge. . . . Nowhere else is direction and expertise . . . more apparent or more critical to the long-term prospect of an organization. As the growing need and transforming competitive environment among organizations increase, organizations will need to be able to identify, recruit, retain, train, and develop the best possible technocrats and leaders to remain competitive.

Organizations require productive technocratic expertise and effective leadership, high technical and tactical knowledge, high social and interpersonal abilities, and political wisdom. In light of the changing and ever-increasing competitive environments, the abilities and skills historically associated with technocrats and leaders require a new process to incorporate accountability. Organizations must move away from subjective criteria when measuring technocratic productivity and leadership effectiveness.

Measuring technocratic productivity and leadership effectiveness through validated survey instruments provides a valuable professional training and organizational development tool allowing organizations to develop and objectively measure the actual effect of technocratic expertise and leadership development initiatives. By measuring and continually improving technocratic productivity and leadership effectiveness, organizations' working environments, output, profitability, and job satisfaction would improve. Of importance, this analytical theoretical observational analysis in this book is intended to highlight that technocratic and leadership attributes contribute significantly to organizations' productivity, effectiveness, output, and job satisfaction. Thus, only through actual objective measure of technocratic productivity and leadership effectiveness can organizations accurately determine the impact and relevance of their professional development and training programs.

Theoretical Description of Vital Expressions

Several terms in this book are somewhat general in nature, such as leadership, which is commonly understood as "a process whereby intentional influence is exerted by one person over other people to guide, structure, and facilitate activities and relationships in a group or organization" (Yukl, 2002, p. 2).

Nevertheless, numerous definitions of leadership have been provided depending upon the researcher's particular area of interest and area of focus. An early definition by Hemphill (1959) focused on the behavior of leaders to direct the activities of others toward common goals. A definition of the early promoters of charismatic leadership styles established leadership as an act that, when exercised, mobilizes resources to arouse, engage, and satisfy the motives of subordinates (Burns, 1979). A more recent definition by House (1996) characterizes leadership as the ability of an individual to influence, motivate, and enable others to contribute toward the effectiveness and success of the organization. However, a common theme is present in most definitions of *leadership*. This theoretical analysis revolves around this definition.

However, other expressions or terms are used that are much more concise and specific to the analysis or perspective in this book. Expressions or terms such as *technocratic* or *technocrat* refer to a group of experts or specialists within an organization that specialize in a specific field of study, profession, or discipline (American Heritage Dictionary of the English Language, 2012). According to Funk and Wagnalls College Dictionary (1974), technocrats are "an organized body of experts." This book adopts the American Heritage Dictionary definition.

CHAPTER 2

An Antiquated Perception of Personality and Work

Perceptions of work have not changed fundamentally as fast as those of organizations. Over the decades, conventional ideas for distinguishing organizational structures and strategies have proliferated. Adhocracies (Mintzberg, 1979), networked organizations (Powell, 1990), virtual organizations (Byrne, 1993), shamrock organizations (Handy, 1989), and lean structures (Womack, Jones, and Roos, 1990) are but a partial list. Many have come from studies of organizations in technical and service organizations, the cutting edge of the postindustrial economy. In sharp contrast, we continue to think about work, even in technical and service settings, with concepts and categories discovered during the Second Industrial Revolution or before. The possibility that current concepts for envisioning work are more antiquated than our thinking of organizations is suggested by the formal systems used to classify occupations, the cultural dichotomies used to distinguish types of work, and the type of occupations that lurk in the background of established theories.

Official Classifications: Most occupational sociologists agree that the detailed occupational classifications by which the U.S. government categorizes jobs are antiquated (Spenner, 1979, 1983; Miller et al., 1980; Attewell, 1990; Steinberg, 1990). Since 1939, the Department of Labor has only incrementally revised the Dictionary of Occupational Titles (DOT), which represents the best source of data on the content of jobs in the U.S. economy. As a result, analysts can make much finer distinctions among manual work than among managerial, clerical, service, sales, professional, or technical work. Cain and Treiman (1981) reported that 76 percent of the listings in the most recent edition of the DOT (U.S. Department of Labor, 1977) cover manual jobs. Yet only 26 percent of all employed Americans are manual workers, a decline of 14 percent since 1940. Seventy-two percent are employed in some form of administrative or service work (an increase of 28 percent since 1940), and the remainder (2 percent) are in agricultural labor. Thus, researchers are forced to chart occupational trends with categories developed for an economy that existed somewhere between twenty-five to fifty years ago.

Cultural Differences: Even more problematic is the fact that our everyday concepts for talking about work are relics of the Industrial Revolution. Differences such as manual and administrative, mental and manual, worker and manager, and even the more jurisdictional, exempt and nonexempt, are the custom of a world in which one's status rested largely on whether one's job involves sitting in the office or toiling under the elements all day. Although these distinctions are still vital, their usefulness vanishes with each passing year. For example, low-skilled service jobs may be just as unattractive as manufacturing jobs; however, they cannot be simply categorized as manual in the conservative sense of the term. The distinction between manager and worker also less adequately signals the nature of a person's work and status than it once did. Workers today are as likely to be engineers or programmers as they are machinists. Managers and administrators are as likely to have no employees as they are hundreds. Yet because these concepts have shaped formal as well as everyday theories of work, researchers who study the workforce and the workplace continue to spin out analyses predicated on their usefulness, usually with less than satisfactory results. For example, attempts to extend deskilling theory to occupations like programming (Kraft, 1979) have proven questionable (Kuhn, 1989), largely because it is arduous to explain convincingly how implementation could be separated from cognition in lines of work that had little manual content from the start.

Pure-Types: Personality images that structure our theoretical and intuitive grasp of the division of labor are also becoming outdated; just as one can speak of pure-types that inform our thinking about organizations (Weber, 1968), so can one speak of pure-typical personalities. A pure-typical personality is an abstraction that captures key attributes of a cluster of personalities. As Weber noted, pure-types are useful not because they are descriptively accurate—actual instances rarely demonstrate all of the attributes of a pure-type—but because they serve as models that assist in thinking about social phenomena. In much the same way that

Weber used the ideal of a bureaucracy to establish his theory of industrial society, occupational sociologists have employed images of pure-typical personalities as anchors for fashioning theories of management and work. Pure-typical personalities are also useful in everyday life, where they structure lay images of the division of labor. Employees in manufacturing organizations are one such pure-type. It invokes images of individuals in manufacturing organizations standing beside a swiftly moving conveyor, repeatedly performing the same operation on each assembly that flows by. Boredom, fatigue, routine, lack of autonomy, and little need for thought or education are the hallmarks of such work. Although manufacturing jobs have always been more varied than this, the pure-type nevertheless evokes a constellation of attributes that capture the family resemblance among many manufacturing jobs. The clerk, the leader, the technocrat, the leader, and the secretary have prominent pure-typical personalities.

Pure-type personalities are professionally and theoretically useful. By reducing the diversity of work to a few modal images, pure-types assist us both in comprehending how the division of labor is structured and in assigning status to individuals. They help parents shape their children's aspirations. They provide designers of equipment with images of users. They assist sociologists in developing formal models of attainment. It is not clear how we could think in general terms about worlds of work without such anchors. The problem is that pure-type occupations are temporarily amalgamated.

More essentially, in an era of extensive economic and technological change, understanding the transforming nature of personality and work is essential to understanding organizing and reorganizing. As Scott (1981) explains, most of modern organizational theory focuses on an organization's relation with its environment. Although economic pressures, institutional transformations, and population dynamics certainly shape organizational strategies and structures, organizations must still make choices about how to organize systems of work effectively to remain viable. Simply acknowledging that work is becoming more complex or interdependent does not describe a changing mode of production. Without answers to questions about what is done, how knowledge is distributed, and how exigencies of work and relations of production are structured, organizational theorists risk telling incomplete and even inaccurate stories about these choices and how and why organizations should change. For example, most commentators portray teams, discuss hierarchies, and network structures as ways to contribute and sometimes response to environmental turbulence, lower labor or transaction costs, enhance commitment, increase flexibility, and so on. Such accounts are certainly reasonable not only because they are consistent with previous organizational theory but also because they reflect the rhetoric that surrounds experimentation with such structures in organizations.

Yet, because these accounts gloss over the issue of how work might be transformed, they neglect the prospect of a deeper cause of transformation that may partly explain why such structures facilitate the abovementioned possibilities. Suppose that work was transforming such that expertise was becoming more technical, more unevenly distributed, and less readily formalized or rationalized. Under such conditions, society might witness the resurrection of lines of work organized along occupational rather than administrative lines (Freidson, 1973). Hierarchical bureaucracy have become less effective modes of structuring not simply because the environment had become more turbulent but because authority of expertise and authority of position have become deficiently amalgamated. In the remainder of this reflective theoretical observational analysis, I argue that this is precisely the implication of the emergence of technocrats' work. Although one can point to numerous lines of work that capture an important aspect of the transforming division of labor, no applicant for the status of an occupation that is pure-type of broad transformations in the nature of work in the late twenty-first century is more credible than the technocrat.

CHAPTER 3

Technocrat: a Pure-Type

To begin with, organizational theory's silence about work can be explained historically. One can argue that studies of work are simply not part of the field's mandate. When organization theory broke from industrial sociology in the 1960s, its originators discarded the study of work to solidify their jurisdictional claim (Bailey, 1996). As Bailey explains, work developed into the academic property of organization theory's sister discipline, the sociology of work and occupations. Because early organizational theorists were dedicated in search of universal principles of organizing, when they found it essential to talk about work, they turned to generalizations. With concepts like complexity and uncertainty, researchers hoped to level distinctions between work as dissimilar as management and the medical field so as to discover relations that would hold across contexts. Moreover, the methods that organizational theorists preferred made it difficult to acquire direct knowledge of work practices. Cross-sectional surveys, lab experiments, secondary data, and interviews with top managers, in effect, distanced analysts from the details of work. Yet, as attractive as these justifications may be, if one could alter history to expunge them, it is still unclear that organizational theorists could currently come to terms with changes in the nature of work. This is because of the field's failure to grapple with work; this also reveals a more subtle deficiency that is not organizational theorists' alone. It also reveals an outdated perception of work.

Current Professional Recognition: The terms *technocrat* and *technician* have completely similar meanings in the English language. Hence, the word *technician* is a relatively recent addition to the language of occupations.

Although the term entered the English language from French early in the nineteenth century, it initially carried no professional connotation. To be a technician in the nineteenth century was simply to be "skilled in the technique or mechanical part of an art, as music or painting" (Oxford English Dictionary, 1989). Nor was the word particularly flattering: it implied a capable practitioner with no creative talent. By the early twentieth century, *technician* had acquired its initial association with work. Most dictionaries of the time defined *technician* as a person versed in the technical aspects of any subject, including *practical arts*, a nineteenth-century term for craft. Thus, according to Funk and Wagnalls College Dictionary, the term *technician* means one who performs tasks that require specialized knowledge. Similarly, the word *technocrat* originated from the term *technocracy* basically meaning "a theory of society and government that advocate the control of experts." Therefore, technocrats in modern public organizations are "experts" if, by virtue of their expertise, they are responsible for the contributions that materially and tangibly affects the capacity of organizations to perform and to obtain results. This may be the capacity of an organization to serve the public efficiently and effectively or to bring out a new product or service in the same manner. Technocrats are responsible for their contributions. And by virtue of their expertise, they are supposed to be better equipped to make the right decision than any other individual within an organization. Technocrats' operational vision can be overruled by senior administrative or managerial leaders. But as long as a technocrat is expected to perform, the specialized operational goals, the standards, and the contributions are his or her responsibility.

Connection to Modernism: Etymology also shows that *technocrat*'s modern meaning is tightly tied to management, administration, science, and technology. In fact, the spread of electronics and technology in public organizations probably offer technocrats their legitimacy within modern organizations. Over the years, when *technocrat* first appeared in the subject headings of television news, the term was routinely cross-referenced with high-level officials in one or more United Nations–specialized organizations as well as high-level political appointees within the United States government. Most references about technocrats on television or radio news in this era discussed expert career opportunities in administration, management, electronics, technological, and politics. The link to high political and professional careers are further substantiated by the fact that most people who are technocrats within organizations work in administration, management, technology, electronics, and political contexts. Thus, the emergence of technocrat as a professional personality trait and title seems to reflect some of the same broad forces that have led organizational theorists to hypothesize the need for new forms of organizing.

Growth in Technocrats' Occupations: The technocrat's candidacy for the status of a pure-type is further supported by the growth of technocratic occupations over the years. In 1950, 1 percent of all employed Americans were involved in some form of technocratic occupations (Szafran, 1992). By 1990, the percentage had grown to 3.4 percent, and the Department of Labor has estimated that the percentage will rise to nearly 4 percent by the middle of the next decade (Silvestri and Lucasiewicz, 1991). While technocratic occupations have grown tremendously through the years, as observed by the number of specialist positions in local, state, and federal governments, technocrats' contributions within public and private organizations are still grossly underestimated, but they are hardly insignificant. In the broader scheme of things, technocrats outnumber leaders within organizations worldwide. Public and private organizations currently comprise more technocrats than ever existed worldwide. According to the Bureau of Labor Statistics, the proportion of Americans employed within technocratic occupations have grown over 240 percent since the midcentury, a rate that outnumbers the expansion of all other occupational clusters charted by the bureau.

Official statistics on the growth of technocratic occupations probably underestimate actual growth rates or are nonexistent. The government usually does not count certain occupations as technocratic; it counts only workers of well-established occupations as such. Sometimes, governments only consider only well-known low-skilled occupations—mechanics, repair persons, and carpenters—as technocrats. Thus, other occupations, such as analysts, engineers, administrative or operational specialists, and even politicians are grouped beneath the rubric of precision production, craft, and repair occupations. Computer operations are usually considered administrative support occupations. More importantly, official occupational categories are blind to trends that are bringing technocratic work to organizations.

The Technocratization of Work: Technocratic occupations involve a myriad of occupations not associated with scientific or technical work. Although some organizations have basically renamed their workers "specialists" to counter the threat of unionization (Whalley and Barley, 1996), there is reason to believe that the occupation title's growing popularity also indexes substantive transformation. After a decade of predictions that computer technologies would displace clerks and workers in the manufacturing organizations (Braverman, 1973; Glenn and Feldberg, 1979; Crompton and Reid, 1982; Noble, 1984), evidence collected since the early 1980s suggests that a more widespread scenario may be the outright elimination rather than the displacement of some occupations, coupled with the enhancement of skill levels of the jobs that remain (Hirschhorn, 1984; Attewell, 1987; Zuboff, 1989; Adler, 1992). This technocratization of work, as it might be called, appears to proceed along two paths.

The First Path Is Demographic: As organizations adopt technologies, employment shifts to more specialized and technical occupations. Studies on office automation within public and private organizations indicate that the shift is a joint product of two trends: computers allow organizations to employ fewer workers, but organizations must hire more programmers, systems analysts, and computer technicians (Attewell, 1987; Baran, 1987; DiPrete, 1988). Milkman and Pullman (1991) report similar transformations in manufacturing that adopt advanced automation: manual and semispecialized work disappears while the number of specialists or technocrats grows. Thus, technological systems seem to shift the expertise level within organizations higher by eliminating low-level tasks and moderately expanding the number of technocrats within organizations. The ultimate outcome was of glimpse in Japan, where organizations embraced technology-integrated processes earlier than in the United States. The Japanese workers observed manufacturing organizations staffed by large numbers of robots tended exclusively by a handful of technocrats (Ruzic, 1981).

The second path entails a transformation of existing tasks and relations of service and production: the reeducation of the workforce. Most evidence of reeducation come from observational studies within organizations that have acquired advanced electronic technologies. Zuboff (1989) claims that the technologies have "informated" the operatives' work. By this, she means that their work has become more abstract, more symbolic, more focused on the intricacies of instrumentation and increasingly distanced from its physical and sensory referents. Others who study computer-integrated manufacturing routinely have reached similar conclusions (Hirschhorn, 1984; Majchrzak, 1988; Kern and Schumman, 1992). The scenario is reminiscent of observations made in the 1950s and early 1960s by industrial sociologists who have studied continuous process operations, where automated controls were first widely employed and where the term *technician* was first applied to factory work (Mann and Hoffman, 1960; Blauner, 1964; Faunce, 1965). But informated work does not appear to be confined to those who work in continuous process environments. There is evidence that advanced electronics and computational technologies have made the work of some technicians such as radiological technologists (Barley, 1990), engineers (Nelsen, 1996b), electronic specialists (Shaiken, 1984), other specialized crafts (Keefe et al., 1992), and even office workers (Zuboff, 1989; Taitro, 1992) more abstract, more complicated, and in some cases more tightly linked to formal technocratic or specialized process. Thus, technocratic work appears to be typical of broader trends in the workplace.

Contravening Professional Categories: The most convincing reason for treating technocrats as a new pure-type may be that they systematically violate society's concepts of making social sense of work. Technocrats are administrators, superintendents, managers, mathematicians, scientists, computer scientists, and more. Yet they use tools and instruments, work with their hands, make objects, repair equipment, and, from time to time, get dirty. Like those with higher status, technocrats have considerable autonomy and are often trusted and relied upon for organizational growth, though sometimes grudgingly, by leaders (Zabusky and Barley, 1996). With the exception of some leaders, technocrats usually work in some of the most highly educated occupational category (Carey and Eck, 1984). Yet, like midlevel employees, technocrats are often paid less than leaders and are accorded low status within public and private organizations (Franke and Sobel, 1970; Keefe and Potosky, 1996; Orr, 1996). Technocrats thus violate the alignment of those attributes that have long distinguished leaders and followers.

Technocrats' Work Is More Respectful of Existing Pure-Types: Table 1 depicts technocrats with respect to their professional characteristics that sociologists usually attribute to them, pure-type occupations that previous researchers have used to make sense of the technocratic roles (Even, 1964; Roberts et al., 1972; Koch, 1977). Technocrats' personality, operations, and responsibilities are sufficiently realistic and technical that individuals outside their category can claim to possess the same skills or knowledge. Their personality and abilities are relatively unique and often requires specialized education or training to enhance their skills. Some technocratic occupations have even developed occupational societies and journals. Yet, in other ways, technocrats' work more closely resembles blue-collar work.

Technology, practitioner education, and scientific and technical training play a crucial role in the education of technocrats (Carey and Eck, 1984), and a significant number of technocrats are highly educated through formal education with graduate and postgraduate degrees (Smith, 1987). Moreover, some technocrats operate equipment, create relics, and possess valued manual skills. Usually, certification and other forms of documentary control over entry are paramount. Finally, technocrats at a certain level are more likely not involved in unions as they are viewed as professionals, a tendency that is especially strong within United States public organizations.

Table 1: Professional Characteristics of Technocrats

Professional Characteristics of Technocrats	Elements
Nature and allocation of knowledge and abilities	Knowledge and ability are solid and well shielded. Few outsiders have more than slight understanding of the content of the discipline's knowledge base. They are considered experts or practitioners in their disciplines.
Intellectual, logical, physical, and sensate duties and responsibilities	Duties and responsibilities are heavily weighted toward the intellectual and logical. Some levels of technician discipline require a significant manual component.
Importance of formal education for recognition and participation	Required undergraduate degree, specialist certification, or graduate degree. Some levels require specialized associate degree or its equivalent or on-the-job training.
Validation of concrete professional achievement	Accreditation boards, licenses, professional journals. Some levels only require job experience or client recommendation.
Importance of on-the-job training	Not important for evidence at certain level but very important for proof of on-the-job experience.
Formal certification required to practice	Vital requirement to substantiate expertise. Some levels only require verification of job experience.

Professional means of controlling admission	Verification of credentials, verification of licenses, supporting documents, and recommendations.
Proclivity to unionize	Very low at some levels and high at other levels.
Professional classifications	Administrators, analysts, specialists, superintendents, political operatives, advisers. Administrative tech, dental tech, computer tech, registered nurse, procurement tech, and more

Faced with this blurring of professional and occupational categories, the few sociologists who have studied technocrat occupations have sought to resolve these anomalies by forcing technocrats into one category or the other or by relegating them between categories. The first approach was favored by Marxists in the 1960s and 1970s who thought they saw in technocrats (technicians) a challenge to existing class structures. The resolution's inadequacy quickly surfaced in an extended argument between those who saw technocrats as members of a new working class (Mallet, 1975) and those who felt they were a new middle class (Poulantzas, 1978; Gorz, 1982). In the end, the new class debate settled on a mundane compromise: technocrats were an intermediate class (Roberts et al., 1972; Smith, 1987). From the start, locating technocrats in the space between analytic categories was the preferred solution of American sociologists of occupations.

Following Etzioni (1969), some sociologists classified technocrats as semiprofessionals, members of occupations who had some but not all of the characteristics of leaders. Others treated them as members of marginal occupations, implying that their work was neither quite a technique nor quite a leadership position and, hence, that they were subject to status inconsistencies (Evans, 1964; Koch, 1977).

The problem with such resolutions is that sociologists tell us more about the difficulty of discarding traditional analytic categories than about technocrats. Rather than take blurred concepts as evidence that technocrats are somehow marginal to the existing division of labor, one might argue that the blurring suggests a work role that challenges the utility of existing ways of thinking. Under this hypothesis, if one is to understand technocrats' work and its implications for implementing, analyzing, producing, and organizing, one must build a model of technocrats' work based on an understanding of what technocrats do. It was to achieve such an understanding that I endeavored to write this reflective theoretical observational analysis about the different occupational attributes I observed in the military and in public service. Thus, table 2 below depicts the contrasting personality traits of technocrats and leaders.

Table 2: Contrasting Personality Traits of Technocrats and Leaders

Technocratic Work	Governance
Self-motivated	Motivate others
Purposeful	Inspired purpose
Self-directed	Create direction
Narrow organizational responsibility	Broad organizational responsibility
Responsibilities are practical	Responsibilities are conceptual
Governed by facts and principles of the discipline	Governed by organizational rules and regulations

Chapter 4

Theoretical Perspectives on Technocratic Work and Governing

Technocratic attributes and work have not been influenced and have not been viewed in terms of the historic perspective of governance, which has been defined as either "initiating structure," which involve control of processes, task development, and workflow organization, or "consideration," which involve the development of emotional relationships. No complete technocratic model has been established to challenge perspectives on governance that can define attributes that fall into various technocratic categories. Technocratic work is about mobilizing resources to perform productively and transforming organizations' resources into accomplishments, specializations into practicalities, ingenuities and unproductivity into productivity, and imagination into opportunities.

On the other hand, models on governance have been linked with the Ohio University study on governance that defined *governance* as either an "initiating structure" (control of processes and organization) or "consideration" (emotional concern for subordinates). While the Ohio University study and later the Michigan University study of the 1950s provided much of the foundation for modern research on governance theories, most models on governance have failed to fully capture or identify specific characteristics of governing. In addition, many of the models could not hold up to scientific and statistical scrutiny. In order to justify, incorporate, and identify a more comprehensive and wider range of leadership behaviors and traits, researchers have increased their research effort on governance significantly over the years and ignored any other organizational personality or traits.

Historical perspective on governance models have related governing to initiating structure that provide consideration to subordinates. The historical perspective on governance can be grouped into four categories: universal approach to governing, characteristics of followers and circumstances, comprehensive theories on governance, and a comprehensive transactional model.

Governing approaches or models can be explored within the context of the three governing approaches that have served as major outline for examining various governing models such as attribute approach, decision-making approach, governing irrelevance or implicit governing theory, vertical relationship, and contingency approach.

The failure of governing models to fully explain and capture governing attributes prompted the development of a self-described full-range governing model by Avolio and Bass (2002) in the mid-1980s that incorporated a variety of governing characteristics. Various governance models have been developed to challenge traditional models, initiate intellectual stimulation, and broaden the scope of governing attributes and styles. Transactional and transformational leadership theories represent modern perspectives with intensive academic research to include case studies, field studies, and laboratory studies (Avolio & Bass, 2002; Dvir, Eden, Avolio, & Shamir, 2002).

Theoretical Perspectives on Technocratic Operational Process

Within modern organizations, we must be talking about productive technocrats; technocrats owe their organizations productivity. There are five practices that contribute to productivity: recording where a technocrat invests his or her time, concentrating on contribution, making strength productive, doing first things first, and making productive decisions.

Recording Where a Technocrat's Time Goes: This is mechanical or otherwise mechanistic. Technocrats do not have to do this by themselves; they can delegate the responsibility of identifying their time to their office assistant. Even if a technocrat identifies where he or she spends his or her time, he or she will make substantial progress, and the outcome of recording his or her time would be fast, if not instantaneous. The continuous recording of a technocrat's time will prod and nudge him or her to proceed to the next activity that would enhance productivity.

The analysis of technocrats' time, the eradication of the needless processes that waste technocrats' time, require them to change the way they function, their associations, and their priorities. Technocrats must always inquire about the relative significance of different activities and objectives that consume unnecessary time. Their activities and objectives must influence the stage and the value of the entirety of work that they perform. However, technocrats must utilize checklists regularly to ensure that they are adhering to their plans. Using checklists regularly enables technocrats to efficiently utilize the most limited of organizations' resources, which is time.

Focusing Attention on Contributions: Technocrats who concentrate on contribution usually advance their attention from procedural to the conceptual, from mechanics to analysis, and from efficiencies to issues about outcomes. Technocrats must rationalize the purpose for which they were hired and what they need to accomplish. They must think and vision their own objectives and norms as well as those of the organization. Those organizational objectives and norms must motivate technocrats to demand high standards of themselves and all around them. Principally, these objectives and norms require that technocrats assume responsibility instead of subordinate themselves to the will of superiors. Technocrats must focus attentively on their own contributions and those of others working on the same or identical projects; they must be attentive in conceptualizing the purpose and outcomes of their projects rather than concentrating on the method of accomplishment alone.

Making Ability Productive: Making ability productive is basically a mindset espoused in deeds. It involves technocrats respecting themselves and others, and in the process, they put their value system in action, "learning through doing," and enhancing themselves personally and professionally through practice. Technocrats who make their abilities productive incorporate their purpose and their organizations' need, their personal capacity and their organizations' outcomes, and their accomplishment and their organizations' opportunities.

Operating in Stages: Technocrats must perform their operations in stages, but the focus is on what needs to be done rather than the time needed to do it. Thus, performing operations in stages does not involve information "but character: foresight, self-reliance, courage." It is about proficiency and not technocratic or specialized brilliance or genius. It is a much more modest yet more enduring technocrat of dedication, determination, and serious purpose.

Making Productive Decisions: There are no specific methods technocrats can use to make productive decisions; however, technocrats can establish distinct measures such as establishing values and direction on how to proceed with organizational tasks. The decisions they make to proceed after they recognize that certain steps might bring about problems to their previous decisions are usually abstract. Technocrats have to address problems on a case-by-case basis; deciding how to address the situation and in what order must be unambiguous. This requires specialized training, procedure, and, most importantly, analysis; it requires an "ethic of action."

There is much more to technocrats' self-development than training in productivity. It involves the attainment of knowledge and skills and a willingness to learn new ways of doing things. Technocrats must also be willing to unlearn some embedded old practices. Even the enhancement of knowledge, skills, and practices would hardly be useful to technocrats unless they first learn how to become productive.

Chapter 5

Technocrats Are Experts

Implementing an organization's functions and operations is the responsibility of technocrats. Producing end products and services and implementing organizations' functions and operations are the same. Whether technocrats work in public or private organizations, they are, first of all, expected to be proficient, productive, knowledgeable, and technically and tactically well grounded at a specific technical or operational organizational task. Simply put, technocrats are expected to be an expert at a specific organizational task.

Thus far, technocrats who are experts are noticeably absent in public and private organizations' structures to a certain extent. Individuals who are very theoretically intelligent are easily found within organizations. Individuals who are governing are mostly intellectual thinkers, and they are far from rare within organizations. These individuals in most cases tend to be high motivators. However, there seems to be a high correlation between technocrats and their intellect, skills, and knowledge.

Individuals in governance positions are usually not technical or operational experts because cleaver perspectives are not by themselves accomplishments. Most of them have never realized that cleaver perspectives only become accomplishments through hard methodical work. Conversely, in every organization, there are some extremely theoretically intelligent individuals in governance positions who are by nature technocrats. Some governors run around hustling-bustling, confusing that action with creativity, but technocrats are hardworking and methodical in their actions.

Intellect, immerse constructive thinking, and understanding of one's task are indispensable resources; nevertheless, only technocrats covert them into outcomes. By themselves, they establish limitations to what an individual can accomplish.

Perspectives on the Conceptual Need for Technocrats: Because individuals have different personalities, abilities, and expertise, organizations will benefit tremendously from the dexterity of technocrats. This is because technocrats' range of knowledge of certain organizational tasks is realistically greater than leaders' technical and operational knowledge.

All this must be apparent. However, little attention has been given to organizational technocrats, in an era in which there are a myriad of books and articles on every aspect of leadership and management.

One perspective for this is that technocrats are usually proficient, knowledgeable, and technically, operationally, and tactically sound at a particular organizational task but are unable to lead or manage individuals because they are unable to create purpose, motivation, and direction for others to follow. In other words, they are usually self-motivated, purposeful, and self-directed to accomplish organizational tasks. Technocrats' abilities are intrinsic whereas leaders have the ability to create purpose, motivation, and direction; they have the ability to project those leadership qualities outward. Governance requires an extrinsic ability. Until now, there is no known study or work that focuses solely on organizational technocrats within organizations.

For the successful implementation of some mental and physical tasks, organizations depend on technocrats, that is, individuals with the aptitude to do things right and systematically in order to get the right task done. Technocrats can always be judged in terms of the quantity and quality of a definable and distinct output. Technocrats' focus is on evaluating productivity and how to characterize quality in some mental and physical tasks within organizations. They are usually preoccupied with multiplying the output of fellow technocrats within organizations.

Previously, technocrats who work within public and private organizations dominated these organizations. More individuals with technocratic skills were needed; technocrats who actually operate and implement organizations' tasks and policies were so many that their duties and responsibilities were taken for granted. People depended on the delivery of goods and services, and technocrats were the few individuals who knew what the rest have to learn the hard way, and that was the effective and efficient accomplishment of tasks.

This factual occurrence was not merely of public and private organizations but also of the military. It is difficult to comprehend in today's world that public organizations around the time of the Civil War in the United States over a century ago comprised of a handful of individuals. President Lincoln's war secretary had less than fifty employees working for him, of which the majority were technocrats who were policy makers. During President Theodore Roosevelt's administration, the entire federal public administration establishment could easily be housed in one of the federal government buildings alongside the present Mall.

Until recently, the foremost quandary of organizations was not technocrats, during the performance of specialized tasks; technocrats did what they were asked to do. Governing positions were not the dominant positions within organizations.

In fact, in the early days, only a minute fraction of individuals were in governance positions within organizations. Majority of the individuals who were in governance positions worked as consultants and on their own as business professionals, at best with one employee. Their governance qualities or lack thereof affected only their businesses.

Currently, however, governance is central to organizations' certainties. Contemporary society possesses a culture of large organizations. The center of gravity is not on technocrats in almost every organization, including the military; it has shifted to individuals who use their brains and personalities to create purpose, motivation, and direction for others to follow rather than being technically proficient, skilled, and using their mental and physical attributes to advance organizations goals and objectives.

On the increase are huge numbers of governing individuals who have been taught to use their understanding, theories, and conceptualization skills instead of their mental, physical, and technical attributes to successfully participate toward enhancing organizations' goals and objectives.

Now organizations cannot take productivity for granted, and it cannot be neglected either. The commanding scheme of measurements and tests that organizations have established for technocrats, from engineering to quality management, is not applicable to leaders. There are few things less appealing, and less productive, to the almighty than technocrats who rapidly turn out beautiful proposals for the wrong tasks. Working on the correct tasks is why I have described these set of workers technocrats and not leaders or managers. The accomplishments of technocrats are usually realistically measured.

Technocrats cannot be supervised closely or in detail. They only need assistance. However, technocrats must be provided with the materials to accomplish organizations' tasks, and they direct themselves toward performance and participation, that is, toward productivity.

A friend of mine once told me that he went to a research and development facility where he saw pictures that depict reputable researchers and inventors on the door; the wall was uncovered except for a sign that reads "Working, the individuals in the building are hard at work developing the next commercial spacecraft to take humans to Mars."

One can indeed be sure that technocrats usually engage in tangible work within public and private organizations, and yet their participation in organizations' goals and objectives is usually underestimated. Accomplishing organizations' tasks is a technocrat's specific duty; it is the technocrat enterprise.

The motivation of technocrats is dependent on their productivity, on their achievement. If productivity is lacking in technocrats' work, their commitment to work and to participate is usually atrophied, and they will just be serving time going through the motions every working day.

Technocrats implement and produce things that are tangible by themselves. They implement and produce substantial products and services whereas individuals in governance positions only present blueprints of ideas, lead individuals, and manage items and information. Standing alone, these things are useless. The smartest ideas if not converted into tangible products, services, action, or activity are meaningless. Technocrats therefore perform tasks that governors cannot perform. Technocrats cannot depend on the blueprints, facts, and information of leaders. They transform them into products or services.

Technocrats are the single most significant factor of productivity through which highly advanced countries and economies become and remain competitive. This is especially true of the United States, and the single resource in respect to which the United States can probably possess a viable advantage is in academics. Individuals may view education in the United States as not up to the standard they expect; however, it is better than anything underdeveloped countries can afford.

Education is the most costly capital investment individuals have ever experienced. A PhD in natural sciences represents about $150,000 to $250,000 of social capital investment. Even an individual who graduated from university without a particular specialized competency symbolizes an investment of $35,000 or more, which only a wealthy nation can afford.

Education is a sector in which the United States, the wealthiest of all nations, has a legitimate advantage, provided it can make the technocrat industrious. Productivity for a technocrat means the capability to accomplish the right tasks.

Conceptual Identification of Technocrats: Technocrats are people dedicated to a specific line of study or profession. Every individual in a modern organization who is dedicated to a single line of some type of physical, technical, mental, or operational work is known as a technocrat by virtue of his or her specializations. Technocrats are responsible for participation that materially affects the capability of organizations to perform and to obtain outcomes. This may be the capability of organizations to bring out original services or products or, in the private sector, to acquire huge shares of a particular market. It may be the capability of nurses to provide bedside care to their patients, and so on. Such nurses must make assessments; they cannot just carry out orders. They must take responsibility for their actions. And, by virtue of their specializations, they are supposed to be better equipped to make correct assessments than anyone else. Technocrats can be overruled; they can be downgraded or relieved from their duties. Nonetheless, the responsibility to perform the job, the objectives, the principles, and the involvement are in their keeping.

Some individuals in governance positions, though a very small number, are technocrats. However, many individuals who are not in governance or technocratic positions are either owning their skills or trying to identify their specific traits, technocratic or leadership. Technocrats within organizations need capable individuals to govern them; these are individuals in positions of authority, accountability, and decision-making.

This reality is perhaps aptly demonstrated by my thoughts during my service in the military and afterward. How, in a bewildered atmosphere of war, does a commander maintain command? I quickly realized that in an environment of war, commanders are the only individuals who are answerable, and if their soldiers cannot respond when they encounter the enemy, the commanders are usually too far away to give orders. Commanders' responsibilities are to ensure that soldiers have the knowledge. Whatever action soldiers take depends on the situation which only they can evaluate. Accountability is always that of the commander; nevertheless, judgment depends on whoever is on the spot. During wartime, almost every soldier is a technocrat.

There are many individuals in governance positions who are not technocrats. Many individuals are subject-matter experts of varying tasks, and frequently of a fairly large number of tasks, and still do not physically and directly contribute to the establishment of products and services within organizations. Most foremen in the manufacturing industries are technocrats. They are supervisors in the literal sense of the word. They are technocrats in that they supervise the work of their assistants. They also have the responsibility for and authority over the direction, content, and the quality of work or the methods of performance. They can be measured and evaluated hugely in terms of quality and productivity by the benchmarks organizations develop.

Moreover, technocrats do not usually have to have individuals working under them. In certain organizations, the individuals who perform market research may have two hundred employees whereas the individuals who perform market research for other organizations may work by themselves with a secretary as their employee. This should make a little difference in participation between the two scenarios. It is an organizational detail. Two hundred employees, of course, can do a great deal more work than one man. However, it does not mean that they produce and participate more.

Technocrats' tasks are defined by quantity, costs, and outcomes. For these, the size of the group and the magnitude of the technical jobs are not even indicators. Having many technocrats working in a research institution endow the outcome with increment of insight, thoughts, and quality that give the organization the potential of rapid growth and access. If so, two hundred technocrats are cheap; however, it is just as likely that the technocrats will be overwhelmed by all the problems two hundred other technocrats bring to the job and cause through their interactions. They may be so busy arguing and bickering at each other so as to have no time for research and for basic decisions. Technocrats may be so busy trying to smooth out organizational strifes that they never ask the question "What is market research?" and as a result may fail to identify vital issues in the operational process, which may eventually cause unproductiveness and the downfall of their organization.

However, technocrats without employees may be equally productive or unproductive. They may be the source of the know-how and vision that make their organization successful. Or they may spend too much of their time searching for details, which can be described as the footnote that the technician mistook for research, seeing and hearing nothing and thinking even less.

Throughout every one of my observations, I have seen individuals who have no employees, and yet they are technocrats. Rarely indeed do I find incidents like that in the military where at any moment, any soldier of an entire squad or company may be called upon to make decisions with a life-or-death impact to the whole squad or company. However, the physicist in the research laboratory who decides to follow one line of exploration rather than another may make the decision that ultimately determines the future of his or her organization. He or she may be the director. However, he or she may also be, and frequently so, an individual with no governing responsibilities; he or she may not even be a fairly junior individual. Equally, the decision to favor one operation over another financially may be made by superiors in the organization. It may also be made by low-ranking individuals. This is true in almost every area within current complex organizations.

I have called technocrats professionals who are expected by virtue of their position or their specialization to perform duties and responsibilities in normal course of their work that have significant impact on the performance and outcome of an entire organization. They are by no means a majority of specialists. For in specialized work too, as in all other areas, there is unskilled work and routine. However, they are a much larger proportion of the total specialized force than any organizational chart may reveal.

This is beginning to be realized, as we witness the many attempts to provide equivalent ladders of recognition and reward for technocrats and aides and for employees' professional contributions. What few yet realize, however, is how many workers exist even in unexciting organizations, including businesses, government agencies, research organizations, laboratories, and hospitals, that have to enhance productivity in order to make significant and irretrievable impact to legitimize the expertise of technocrats. The decisions technocrats have to make are identical to those of individuals in governing positions.

The most junior aide to technocrats whom I have observed may perform similar tasks as the most supervisory technocrats within organizations, that is, planning, organizing, integrating, and measuring or assessing projects. Technocratic aides' range may be quite limited, however, within their specialties; they are still technocrats.

Conversely, technocrats perform different types of tasks within organizations. Technocrats' scope may be quite narrow; however, they are technocrats even if their functions or their names appear neither on the scalar chain nor the organization's telephone directory.

And despite the experience of technocrats or technocratic aides, technocrats are usually knowledgeable and proficient. Many of the illustrations used in this book are from observations and experience of technocrats in government, the military, hospitals, and businesses. The key reason is that these are accessible, are indeed frequently on the public record, and are easily observed. Furthermore, complex organizational operations are more easily observed and analyzed than small operations.

This is not about what individuals in positions of authority do or should do. This is about identifying technocratic personalities and identifying responsibilities and decisions that are intended to add to the performance capability of organizations. It is intended for individuals who are striving to know their true organizational personality trait.

Perspectives on Technocrat Realities: The realities of the technocrats' circumstances both demand technical or operational knowledge and proficiency from them, which usually makes it a little difficult for them to be productive. Unquestionably, unless technocrats work at becoming proficient, the reality of their circumstances usually will thrust them into unproductivity.

Let me briefly illustrate the realities of a technocrat outside an organization to observe the problem. A neurologist by and large has no problem of productivity. The patient who walks in the neurologist office brings with him or her everything to make the neurologist productive. During the time he or she is with the patient, the neurologist as a rule devotes him- or herself to the patient. The neurologist can keep interruption to a minimum. The contribution the neurologist is expected to make is clear. What is vital and what is not is determined by whatever ails the patient. The patient's illness establishes the neurologist's priorities, and the goals and objectives of the neurologist are given: it is to restore the patient to health or at least make him or her more comfortable. Neurologists are usually not known for their capability to organize themselves and their work; however, few of them have much trouble being productive.

Technocrats within organizations find themselves in completely different circumstances. In their circumstances, there are four realities that they cannot manage. These realities are built into technocrats' day and occupation. They have no alternative but to collaborate with the unavoidable. However, every single one of these realities exercises demand toward unproductivity.

One, technocrats' time usually belongs to the current task at hand, and if one attempts to describe technocrats operationally, one would have to characterize technocrats as captive of their tasks. Unexpected occurrences can affect technocrats' time. There appears to be very little any technocrat can do about their time. Technocrats cannot, as a rule, like a neurologist, stick their heads out the door and say to their receptionist, "I won't see anyone for the next two hours." Because one of their directors will call them at any moment, and they can spend the remaining hours addressing issues that do not have any association with the tasks at hand.

Two, technocrats are compelled to keep on producing unless they constructively modify the circumstances in which they live and work. The complaint currently within organizations is that individuals in governing positions still persist in running technical operations even though they are in charge of personnel and other administrative functions. This is attributed to the fact that these individuals get promoted, normally, out of practical and operational work and cannot abandon that adaptive behavior when they assume governance positions. However, an identical complaint is heard in nations where the professional elevation is different. Within some organizations in other parts of the world, a usual route to governing and management is through midlevel secretaries, where workers perform work as generalists. Yet, in most of these countries, organizations' top management officials are criticized just as much for operating as nations that promote individuals out of practical and operational work. However, this tendency is confined to the top within organizations; it pervades the entire governing group. There must be a reason to operate other than professional ladders or even the general perversity of human beings.

The primary issue is the reality around technocrats. Unless technocrats change their realities deliberately, the flow of occurrence will establish what they are concerned with and what they do.

Depending on the flow of work, it is appropriate for the neurologist, who looks up when a patient goes into his or her office, to ask, "What are you doing today?"

"Sir, I have a problem, I have been having severe headaches."

The patient is telling the neurologist what the priority problem is even if the neurologist decides that, upon closer examination, that headache is a fairly minor symptom of a much more fundamental condition where he will do something to get the patient some relief.

However, occurrences seldom reveal anything to technocrats, not to mention the real problem. For the neurologist, the patient's description of what ails him is essential because it is essential to the patient. The organizational technocrats are concerned with much more complex situations. What occurrences are significant and pertinent and what occurrences are merely disruptions, the occurrences by themselves do not indicate. That they are not even symptoms in terms of the patient's narrative is a clue for the neurologist.

If technocrats let the flow of occurrence determine what they do, what they work on, and what they take seriously, they will squander away their working time. Technocrats may be excellent at what they do; however, technocrats will certainly waste their expertise and capabilities and throw away what little productivity they might have accomplished. What technocrats need are conditions that will enable them to engage in strictly significant tasks that involve participations and outcomes even though the conditions are not found in the flow of occurrences.

The third reality that spurs technocrats toward productivity is their assigned tasks within organizations. This means that technocrats are productive only if and when other members of organizations make use of what technocrats contribute. Organizations are mechanisms that add to the capability of various individuals.

Technocrats within organizations take the technical capabilities of others and their own expertise and use them as resources and motivation. Technocrats are seldom in phase with each other specifically because each technocrat has their own expertise and their own issues. One technocrat may specialize in finance or macroeconomics or in training tomorrow's technocrats within an organization whereas the technocrat in the other office is interested in the finer points of microeconomics, home management, or the legalities of urban management. Each has to be able to use the production of the other.

Usually, the workers who are most vital to the productivity of technocrats are not those with whom they work directly. They are workers in other departments, individuals in terms of organization. Or they are the senior technocrats. Unless technocrats can reach these workers, who can make their work productive and that of their organizations, technocrats would likely be unproductive.

Four, in summary, technocrats operate within organizations. Technocrats, whether they are working in a public or private organization, i.e., a research facility, university, or the military, mostly see their organizations internally and as close and immediate certainty. Technocrats see internally through broad and distorted lenses, if at all. They usually do not personally know the externalities of the organization. Technocrats usually comprehend these externalities through an organizational filter of information, which is in an already predigested and highly conceptual form that entails organizational conditions of significance on the outside reality.

However, organizations are concepts. Precisely, they have to be characterized as structures that possess neither dimensions nor expansions. Even well-established organizations are unreal compared to the certainty of the atmosphere in which they operate.

Particularly, there are no outcomes within organizations. All the outcomes are external. The only operational outcomes, for instance, are produced by individuals who transform their efforts and their finances into services, revenues, or profits through their willingness to exchange their monies for services or products. Individuals and taxpayers usually may make their decisions on the basis of economical or market considerations of supply and demand or within a socialist regime which regulate supply and demand on the basis of basically noneconomic value inclinations. In either case, individuals that make vital decisions are usually outside rather than within organizations, i.e., medical facilities have outcomes only in respect to their patients. However, patients are not members of the medical facilities. For patients, medical facilities exist only while they visit or hospitalize. The patients' greatest desire is to go back home as fast as possible.

The occurrences within organizations are human endeavors and expenditures. There are only human endeavor centers. The less work organizations have to perform to produce productive outcomes, the better they will perform their work. If it takes fifty thousand employees to provide a public service or to produce motorcycles for public use, this will be a fundamentally disgusting operational and engineering flaw. The fewer employees, the less action within organizations, the nearly faultless organizations will be in reference to their grounds for survival: their services to communities.

The external aspects of organizations, which are their true realities, are extremely beyond internal productive controls of organizations. At the most, outcomes are codetermined, such as, during wartime, the result of the activities and judgments of both militaries. In private organizations, attempts can be made to shape clients' inclinations and ideals through advertisements and personal ads. Unless in excessive scarce circumstances such as wartime economy, customers still have the final say to accept or reject an organization's product or service. However, it is the internal workings of organizations that are most evident to and have immediacy for technocrats. Their relationships and acquaintances, their issues and challenges, and their cross-currents and rumors get to them at every location within organizations. Unless technocrats make an exceptional effort to gain direct access to external certainties, technocrats will become gradually more focused on internal issues. Conversely, individuals in governing positions usually focus on issues internally and externally within organizations.

Organizations are not like any living thing, an end in itself and thriving by the simple act of perpetuating their kind. Organizations are an appendage of society that fulfills their goals and objectives by the contribution they make to the external environment. And yet the larger and more productive organizations become, the more internal occurrences tend to engage the curiosities, energies, and abilities of technocrats to the exclusion of their real responsibilities and their real external productivity.

This hazard was provoked by the arrival of computer electronics and information technology. Computers, being a mechanical illiterate, can only process quantifiable data speedily, accurately, and precisely. Computers grind out inaccessible quantifiable data in great volumes. Technocrats can only quantify what goes on within organizations, such as productivity figures, statistical data, or training reports. The pertinent external occurrences are seldom available in quantifiable form until it is much too late to do anything about them.

This is not because the information-collection capabilities in respect to external occurrences lag behind the technical capabilities of the computer. If this were the only concern organizations confront, they would just enhance arithmetic efforts; furthermore, electronics has significantly assisted organizations to overcome this mechanical constraint. The issue is rather that the significant and pertinent external occurrences are usually qualitative and not capable of quantification. Occurrences are not facts; on balance, fact is an occurrence which individuals have defined, classified, and, most of all, have provided importance to. In order to quantify a data, technocrats have to possess the idea first. Technocrats have to conceptualize from the perpetual confusion of phenomena a precise feature which they can identify and count.

The actual significant external occurrences are not the trends. They are transformations in the trends. These determine the success or failure of organizations and their efforts. Such transformations, however, can be perceived because they cannot be calculated, described, or categorized. The categorization still generates anticipated numbers.

Computers are logical equipment that have their advantages, but they also have disadvantages. Significant external occurrences cannot be published in the form a computer could possibly handle. Technocrats, nonetheless, while not specifically logical, have perceptions, which are their advantage.

Conversely, technocrats sometimes become disdainful of information and stimulus that cannot be condensed to computer logic and language. Technocrats may become sightless to everything that is perspective rather than fact. Therefore, incredible numbers of computer information may drown out access to certainty.

In all certainty, computers are by far the most useful organizational tool. This should make technocrats aware of their insulation and liberate them to spend time externally. Over time, there has been an acute focus on computers, which has been a serious dilemma.

A computer only makes observable conditions that existed before it. Technocrats by necessity live and work within organizations. Unless technocrats make it their duty and responsibility to recognize the external environment, the internal workings of their organizations may affect their view of true reality.

Technocrats cannot change these four realities. They are necessary conditions for their survival. However, technocrats must therefore assume that they will experience unproductivity unless they make an extraordinary effort to learn to be productive.

Perspective on Technocratic Productivity: Increased productivity may well be the only avenue where technocrats can possibly improve their level of performance, accomplishment, and fulfillment.

Organizations can certainly utilize technocrats of such huge capabilities in many areas. Organizations could use technocrats of broader specializations. Presumably, however, in both of these circumstances, not very much can be anticipated from additional efforts. Organizations may be getting to the position where they are already attempting to do the intrinsically unattainable or at least the unfeasibly unproductive. However, organizations are not going to breed a new race of super technocrats. Organizations will have to operate with technocrats as they are.

Authors on governance, for instance, have imagined perfect individuals of all weather in their vision of individuals who can govern in the future. An individual who can govern, we are told, must possess an astonishing capability as a forecaster and a decision maker. They must possess excellent people skills and understand their organizations and power relationships and have imaginative insights and ingenious thoughts. What seems to be wanted is widespread intelligence, and this widespread intelligence has always been of limited supply. The experiences of individuals reveal powerfully that the only individuals with plentiful supply are the widespread unproductive. Organizations will therefore have to employ individuals who are at best proficient in one of these disciplines. And then they are more than likely to lack the most unassuming gift in the others.

Individuals will have to learn to establish organizations in such a way that individuals who possess ability in a single significant area needed by organizations will have the capability of utilizing it. However, organizations cannot look forward to getting the technocratic performance they need by raising their standards for capabilities, let alone by hoping for universally exceptional individuals. Organizations will have to expand the range of workers through the devices they have to work with rather than through sudden quantum leap of workers' capabilities.

The same, more or less, pertains to technocrats. However, desperate organizations may need workers of more and better expertise, the effort that should be exerted to make the foremost improvement may well be better than any achievable, let alone any plausible, return.

Somewhat less ambitious plans for technocratic improvement call for high specialization in a host of different skills as physics, accounting, finance, economics, and even medicine. Organizations certainly require workers who understand the dynamics of technology, the intricacies of the contemporary world economy, and the web of contemporary government.

Every single one of these is a significant area, indeed, too broad even for technocrats who work on nothing else. Individuals in academia tend to specialize in reasonably limited fragments of the various fields and do not act as if to have more than a journeyman specialization of the field itself. I am not saying that individuals need not try to understand the essentials of other academic areas or disciplines. The fact remains that individuals usually possess expertise in a very small number of disciplines.

This, however, is somewhat especially dissimilar from the generalist, who is as unlikely to occur as general intelligence. Instead, organizations will have to learn how to utilize technocrats who are good in many areas. However, this means enhanced specialization. If organizations cannot augment the supply of resources, they must augment their yield, and productivity is a tool that can make resources of capability and proficiency yield more and better outcomes. Productivity thus deserves high priority as the tool of technocrats and as their entrance to accomplishment and performance.

Perspective on Technocratic Specialization: If human beings were born with certain expertise for a particular task, the way certain people are gifted in dancing or sport, organizations would be in bad shape. For organizations know that only a small minority of individuals possess huge talents in any single professional area. Organizations would therefore be reduced to trying to identify individuals with extreme potential for productivity early and train them as best they can to develop their talents. However, organizations could hardly hope to identify enough individuals for specialized tasks of contemporary civilization this way. Indeed, if productivity were a gift, the current civilization would be extremely susceptible, if not unsustainable, because the current civilization of large organizations is dependent on a large supply of individuals who are competent of being technocrats with a high degree of productivity.

If productivity can be learned, however, three questions arise. What does productivity consist of? What does an individual have to learn? What type of education? It is a skill, and individuals learn these skills in a systematic form and through concepts. It is a skill individuals learn by performing the same task over and over again.

Individuals have been asking questions for every long time. As someone who has worked in the military, government, business, and now in academia, the reality is that productivity is crucial for two reasons. One, as someone who was in the military, and who by definition has some authority over soldiers who are supposed to be specialists at particular tasks, I understand the essence of productivity or else the mission will suffer. Two, the most productive organizations depend on technocrats to get things done. Technocrats' productivity therefore determines whether organizations accomplish positive outcomes or whether organizations are mainly expenditure conscious.

My experiences have taught me that there is no productive personality. The productive technocrats whom I have observed differ widely in their temperament and capabilities, in what they do and how they do it, in their expertise, their interests, in fact in almost everything that distinguishes humanity. All they have in common is the capability to get their work done.

Among the technocrats I know and worked with, there are mostly introverts and detached, retiring individuals; some even are morbidly extroverts. Most are excruciating conformists, some are even unconventional. Some are heavy and some slim, most are relaxed, and some worry a lot. Some abstain from drinking, and some drink excessively. Most are very reserved, some with great charm and warmth.

There are fewer individuals among them who would reply to a popular conception of technocrats. However, there are individuals who would attract no attention within organizations. Some are scholars and serious students, others almost unlettered. Some have broad interests; others know about their narrow area only and care for little else. Some of the individuals are self-absorbed, if not indeed selfish. However, there are some who are charitable of heart and mind. There are technocrats who live only for their work and others whose main interests lie outside, in community work. Among some of the technocrats I have met, there are technocrats who use logic and analysis and others who rely mainly on perception and intuition. There are technocrats who are decisive in what they do and how they do it and those who agonize every time they have to perform within their specialization.

Technocrats, in other words, differ as widely as doctors, professors, and musicians. They differ as widely as do unproductive ones are indeed distinguishable from productive technocrats in style, character, and capacity.

What all these technocrats have in common is the practices that make productive work out of whatever they have and whatever they are. And these practices are the same, whether the technocrat works in a public or private organization, as administrators, or as professors.

However, whenever I observe technocrats, no matter how intelligent, industrious, and proficient they are, I have always rightly identified those that are unproductive.

Productivity, in other words, is a mindset, that is, a multifaceted set of practices. And practices can always be taught. Practices are simple, deceptively so; even a six-year-old would have no problem comprehending a practice. However, practices are usually difficult to do well. They have to learn the same way individuals learn multiplication, for example, which has to be repeated constantly until it becomes a part of the individual, an automatic reflex and a firmly embedded behavior. Practices are taught by repetition.

There is, in so many words, no reason why any individual with average intelligence must not obtain proficiency in any practice. Specialization might well evade some individuals for disciplines that might need special talents. However, what is required to achieve productivity is competency coupled with a structured work ethic, such as the following:

1. Technocrats must identify how they spend their operational-time and how to work methodically at organizing what little of their operational-time they can manage.
2. Technocrats must concentrate on internal participation. They usually work rather than gather their efforts. They frequently start out with identifying their tasks and the results their organizations expect from the tasks rather than figuring out how to perform the task and the techniques and tools required for the task.
3. Technocrats must build on abilities—the abilities of more experienced technocrats and colleagues, less experienced technocrats, and their own abilities in their tasks, that is, on what they can produce. Technocrats should not build on weakness. They should not start out with tasks they cannot perform.
4. Technocrats must focus on a major area where they can produce outstanding results. They must establish priorities and commit to them. Technocrats should know that they have no choice but to perform in stages; otherwise, they will accomplish nothing.

5. Technocrats must make productive decisions. Overall, they must be aware that it is a matter of structure, the right moves in the right order. Technocrats must know that contributions that usually turn out productively usually involve collective effort based on brainstorming rather than on dissenting opinions. They must know that to make many technical decisions hastily means to make wrong decisions, and realize the importance of making few decisions reasonably and constructively, but essentially, they must understand that the right strategy is necessary in making technical decisions rather than hasty tactics. These are the fundamentals of technocrats.

Chapter 6

Technocrats' Time and Task Identification

The majority of discussions about technocrats' work begin with the suggestion that technocrats need to plan their operations. It sounds as if this is supposed to be routine. The only thing is that some technocrats do not practice this routine. Conversely, technocrats' strategic plans do not usually linger within documents that organizations have conceived, nor do they usually stay as good intensions. They usually get accomplished.

Technocrats, in my observation, do not often begin with their work. Most usually begin with their operational-schedule, and they usually start out with planning the work around it. Technocrats usually start by systematically planning their operations, identifying some of the ways they can productively utilize their operational-schedule. They often plot their operational-schedule around their duties and responsibilities and sever unproductive activities. Additionally, technocrats usually merge their operational-schedule into the largest achievable enduring components. They often use a three-step process: logging down operational-schedule, controlling operational-schedule, and merging operational-schedule. These are the foundation of technocrats' productivity.

Most technocrats are aware that their operational-schedules are restrictive features. The operational boundary of most work operations is often established by the most limited resource. In the process, organizations usually describe it as achievement.

Operational-schedule is also an inimitable resource; funds are usually quite abundant within complex organizations. Technocrats often realize that it is the demand for revenue, rather than the supply thereof, which establishes the borderline to economic growth and productivity within organizations. Employees are usually the third restrictive resource organizations can employ although organizations rarely employ enough productive workers. However, they cannot purchase or otherwise acquire more operational-time.

The delivery of operational-time is completely inelastic. Regardless of the extent of the demand, the delivery will not improve. No organization can put a price on operational-time, nor can any economic or statistical curve can be created for it. Furthermore, operational-time cannot completely be unpreserved and cannot be amassed. The operational-time technocrats utilized the prior week is gone forever and can never be recovered. Operational-time is, consequently, constantly in extremely limited supply.

Operational-time is completely unique; within certain limitations, organizations can replace one resource for another, such as capital for individual labor. Organizations can use more specialization or more muscle. However, operational-time can never be replaced.

Every technocrat needs operational-time. It is the single factual widespread situation. Every work takes place within and utilizes operational-time. Usually, most technocrats do not take for granted this exclusive, inimitable, and essential resource. Nothing else possibly differentiates productive technocrats as much as operational-time. Technocrats are usually ill-equipped to control operational-time; regardless how diligent they may be, they are usually unable to control every minute of their operational-time. Technocrats therefore are usually aware that to control their time, they should first know how much operational-time a particular project would entail.

Perspectives on Technocrats Operational-Time and Constraints: There are consistent demands toward inefficient and extravagant usage of time. Regardless of a technocrat's job, every technocrat has spent huge amount of operational-time on things that do not contribute to productivity within their organizations. Much of this operational-time is unavoidably squandered. The more complex the organization, the more demand on technocrats' operational-time.

Likewise, activities that contribute to time wasting abound in the life of every technocrat. When organizations' directors or chairs call on the senior technocrats, they have to respond even if they are busy. Even though there are other important and more pressing issues they have to address, i.e., the nurse supervisor at a hospital has to attend the meeting for every one of her nurses, or else the doctor, the junior nurses, other employees will feel as though they are being slighted. The foremen in service delivery plants had better pay attention when the directors of their organizations call and request for information they need; in a few seconds, the foremen will usually jump on the closest computer to retrieve the information regardless of the task they were performing at the time. So it goes all day long.

Regardless of the position or discipline of an employee within organizations, every employee gets bombarded with demands on their operational-time which adds little, if anything, to their efficiency, and this cannot be ignored.

In almost every technocratic job, a huge aspect of operational-time is often squandered on activities that they clearly have to perform but usually offer little or nothing to their organizations. Although most of the tasks technocrats perform involve operational-time, even the least productive task often consumes a moderately huge amount of operational-time, and expending less than the minimum operational-time on certain tasks can breed unproductivity and will be an absolute waste of operational-time. This is because the technocrat will achieve nothing and will often have to start all over again.

To be productive, every technocrat, as a result, needs to be able to dispose of operational-time in fairly huge portions. It will be inadequate for technocrats to possess little bits and pieces of operational-time even if the total number of hours at the technocrat's disposal is remarkably high. This is predominantly accurate in reference to operational-time spent working with other members of the organization, which is, of course, a quintessential task in the work of technocrats. Humans in general are operational-time consumers; some employees are operational-time squanderers.

To squander a few minutes with other organizational members is basically not profitable. If technocrats want to get anything done, they would have to spend a fairly large minimum operational-time. Technocrats who think that they can discuss the plans, directions, and performance of one of their technicians in twenty minutes—and many technocrats believe they can—are just deceiving themselves. If technocrats want to get to the point of having an impact, they usually need about one to two hours and sometimes more. Furthermore, if technocrats want to develop individual relationships, they often need considerably more operational-time.

Relationships with other technocrats are especially operational-time–consuming. Whatever the reason, whether it is nonexistence of or the obstacle of class and authority between technocrats, or whether technocrats simply take themselves too seriously, technocrats require much larger operational-time demands than other organizational members to convince their superiors as well as their acquaintances. Furthermore, because technocrats' work cannot be measured the way those of other workers can, no one with an organization hierarchy can tell technocrats in a few simple words whether they are performing the right job and whether they are performing it well. However, supervisors can discuss their organizations' standards to their workers if the workers are not performing to such standards. However, those same supervisors often have to sit down with their technocrats and think through with them what should be done and why, before they can even know whether they are performing their tasks satisfactorily or not. And this takes operational-time.

Since technocrats usually direct themselves, they often understand what organizations expect of them and why. They usually understand the work of other technocrats who sometimes have to use their expertise for outputs. For this, technocrats need a good deal of information, discussion, and instruction—everything that usually consumes time. Contrary to common belief, this time demand is made not only on supervisory technocrats but also equally by nonsupervisory technocrats and other workers.

Technocrats often concentrate on the positive outcomes and performance objectives within organizations, and to have any positive outcomes and performance means that technocrats have to reserve operational-time to direct their visions from their work to positive outcomes and from their specialty to the external where performance lies.

Whenever other workers achieve excellent performance within complex organizations, technocrats usually invest time from their regular schedules to assist these other workers, sometimes all the way down to the most junior workers. Technocrats usually ask several questions. What should technocrats at the top of the operational or production process know about the process? What should organizations need to tell them regarding the operational or production process? Where do they see opportunities that have not yet been exploited? Where do organizations' leaders see shortfalls to which they as technocrats can't see? And, altogether, what do organizations' governing teams want to learn from technocrats about the operational or production process?

This exchange is paramount equally in government agencies, businesses, research facilities, and in the military. Without this interaction, technocrats and other workers either lose passion or become time investors, or they direct their energies toward themselves, protecting their career and drifting away from operational productivity, opportunities, and the needs of organizations. However, such sessions take huge amounts of time, especially as it is supposed to be unrushed and in a relaxed environment. Everyone involved in this process must feel as though they have enough time to discuss their issues. This essentially means that everyone gets a great deal done quickly, and it also means that they have to allocate huge amounts of time to one meeting and avoid too much interruption.

Combining personal relationships and work relationships contribute to operational-time wasting. If rushed, it turns into resistance. Technocrats often depend on this combination. However, the more individuals interact, the more operational-time their total interaction will take, and the fewer operational-time will be available for them for work, achievements, and outcomes.

Leadership literature has long known the theory of "the span of control," which emphasizes that an individual can lead only few individuals if these individuals have to come together in their own work. On the other hand, technocrats within organizations usually work together from different organizational locations so that any number of technocrats can conceivably report to one departmental governing team or to another organization without violating the "span of control" principle. Whether this theory is valid or not, there is little doubt that the more technocrats who have to work together, the more time they will spend on interaction rather than on work and achievements. Complex organizations create strength by lavishly using their technocrats' time wisely.

The size of the organization, consequently, dictates the actual operational-time technocrats have, and the more significant it will become for technocrats to know how they spend their operational-time and to control the little operational-time they have at their disposal.

The more workers technocrats oversee, the more frequently decisions on individual activity arise. However, fast technical decisions are likely to be erroneous. The time quantum of a good technical decision is amazingly large. What a technical decision entails often becomes transparent only when technocrats have experienced the same issue several times.

Among technocrats I have observed, there have been those who make technical decisions fast and those who make them rather deliberately. However, without exception, they make technical decisions gradually, and they make them several times before they actually obligate themselves to those decisions.

Very many technocrats make technical decisions that impact their organizations. However, technocrats I have observed have learned that they have to give several hours of constant and uninterrupted thought to discussions on operational or production processes if they hope to become successful or productive.

Enough, constant, and nonstop allocation of operational-time is needed for specific technical problems: what responsibilities to assign to workers of a new operational or production process or to new workers of old operational or production process, whether to promote into a vacancy a worker who possesses the skill needed for the operation but lacks enough technical training, or whether to put in a first-rate worker without enough job experience. And so on.

Decisions related to workers are usually operational-time–consuming, for the simple reason that the almighty did not create individuals as resources for organizations. Humans do not come in the proper size and shape for the tasks that have to be performed within organizations, and they cannot be transformed or machined for these operations. Individuals usually adapt at best. Performing the job with other individuals when no other resources are available requires lots of operational-time, thoughts, and judgments.

The operational-time demands on technocrats are not dwindling. Technocrats and workers usually have limited numbers of hours to work and soon may even work fewer hours and live better than anyone has ever lived before, no matter how much they worked or how rich they were. However, workers' spare operational-time is inescapably being paid for by technocrats' longer hours. It is not technocrats who have the problem of spending their spare operational-time in advanced countries. On the contrary, technocrats are working longer hours in almost every parts of the globe and have greater demands on their operational-time to be successful and productive for their organizations. Technocrats' scarce operational-time will only get worse rather than better.

A significant basis for this is that an improved standard of living presumes an economy of modernization and transformation. However, modernism and transformation make inordinate operational-time demands on technocrats. What technocrats can think and do in the near future is to think about what they already know and do as individuals have always done.

Because of these reasons, the demand on technocrats and on workers and the operational-time demands for transformation and modernism have become increasingly vital for technocrats to be able to control their operational-time. However, organizations cannot even think of controlling technocrats' operational-time unless they are aware of where it goes.

Perspectives on Technocrats' Operational-Time Identification: Technocrats must document their time in order for them to identify how much operational-time they have and how to use it; in return, technocrats usually endeavor to manage their operational-time, which is supposed to be the case throughout every individual's professional life. Organizations have recognized this as it relates to hourly workers. Ever since organizations started utilizing Fredrick Taylor's Scientific Management in the 1900s, organizations have required workers to document their operational-time.

Hardly any advanced country is behind in operational or manufacturing methods as not to methodically time the operations of certain employees. Organizations have applied the understanding to their operations where time does not hugely matter; that is, where the disparities between time used and time wasted are principally productivity and expenditure.

However, technocrats have not applied this organizational knowledge to the operations that increasingly matter, and that specifically has to deal with operational-time: the duties of every worker and especially those of technocrats. In this case, the difference between operational-time utilized and operational-time squandered is productivity and outcomes. The first step toward technocrats' productivity is therefore to document actual operational-time utilization.

There are particular methods in which the operational-time recorded and organized needs to be addressed. There are technocrats who keep such records. In some organizations, the secretary keeps the records for the organization. The significant thing is that it gets done and that the record is made in actual time of a specific operation rather than afterward on recollection.

Large numbers of productive technocrats usually keep such recorded logs constantly and check them monthly. At the least, some technocrats have their recorded logs run themselves for five to six weeks at a stretch twice annually or so, on a normal schedule. Subsequent to reviewing the work logs, they usually reorganize and modify their schedules. However, usually, during the middle of the year, some technocrats usually realize that they have strayed or squandered huge amount of their operational-time on operational details. Operational-time consumption does not evolve with practice. However, only consistent efforts at controlling operational-time can thwart straying.

Methodical operational-time accumulation is hence the next step. Technocrats have to identify the inefficient, operational-time–squandering behaviors and dispose of them if they possibly can. This entails self-inquiry by technocrats and involves certain specific actions.

First, technocrats must try to recognize and eradicate activities that need not to be performed at all, activities that are clearly wasting operational-time without producing any outcome whatsoever. To identify the activities that reduce technocrats' operational-time, they often require that all operational and production activities be documented in an operational-time log. These activities usually involve the repercussion of ignoring certain tasks, and if no task that will interfere with other organizational operations is present, technocrats usually cease keeping operational-time logs.

It will be astonishing to know the many inconsequential activities where technocrats' participation is required. For instance, the innumerable meetings and seminars that take an uncountable number of technocrats' operational-time, which they really enjoy being a part of, are continued every year. Actually, all technocrats have to do is to speak up if certain activities do not contribute to productivity or enhance the operation or productivity of the organization in any way.

I have yet to see any technocrat, in spite of his or her position in an organization, who has not participated in an insignificant operational endeavor that demands about a quarter of his or her operational-time.

For years, there have been numerous conversations about task delegation within organizations. Technocrats regardless of organization—public, private, universities, or the military—have been urged to delegate better. In fact, most technocrats in complex organizations have taken upon themselves to exhort subordinates to do a better job delegating. I have yet to observe any progress from all the exhortations. The reason why individuals don't listen is simple: as frequently explained, delegating makes almost no sense. If it means that one individual should perform another's task, it is wrong. Individuals are paid to perform their own task, and if the implication is that, as the usual exhortation does, the laziest technocrat is the best technocrat, it is not only gibberish; it is also ethically wrong.

However, I have never observed a technocrat confronted with his or her operational-time log who has not automatically transferred the responsibility to someone else that he or she need not perform personally. The initial glance of the operational-time log will make it apparently transparent that there is just insufficient operational-time to perform tasks the technocrat deems vital, directly want to perform, and which the technocrat is dedicated to perform. The only way a technocrat can get to the significant things is by transferring tasks that can be performed by others.

Thus, I have observed that the most effective way to get rid of inconvenient technocrats in positions of responsibility is to make a world traveler. The airplane is underrated as an organizational tool. Many trips have to be made by senior technocrats; usually these trips are delegated to junior technocrats. Traveling is usually a novelty for new technocrats. They are still young to get a good night's rest in hotel beds. It is assumed that the junior technocrats can cope with the exhaustion, and they will consequently do a better job than the seasoned veteran, possibly with more knowledge, but exhausted.

By the way, there are scheduled meetings to attend although nothing important is going on that no other technocrat can perform. There are also numerous hours spent conversing about a particular project prior to the initial draft. As an illustration, there is in the library the time spent by a senior researcher to compile an admired news release on some of his new biochemistry research. Hitherto there are not many individuals around with adequate chemistry knowledge to comprehend what the researcher is trying to say, who can write understandable English, whereas the researcher can only converse in advanced chemistry. On the whole, in a massive quantity of the work being performed by technocrats, this is work that can simply and consequently be performed by others.

Delegating, as the term is usually used, is widely misinterpreted; those who do misinterpret it are indeed misguided. However, getting rid of anything that can be performed by some other individual so that someone else does not have to delegate but can really get to his or her own work is a key improvement in productivity.

A general cause of operational-time wasting is mostly under technocrats' control and can be eradicated by them, and that is by wasting the time of other technocrats. However, there is no solid proof that such things happen. Nonetheless, there is still an uncomplicated way to know, which is inquiry with other technocrats. Productive technocrats have learned to inquire methodically and without shyness about the activities that squander their time without affecting productivity.

The approach technocrats usually employ to become productive may still be a serious waste of another technocrat operational-time. Usually, senior technocrats of complex organizations are absolutely well aware that the meetings in their offices waste a lot of operational-time. I observed a team leader who requested that every subordinate working directly for her attend every meeting, regardless of the topic. As a result, the meetings were far too large. Because every employee felt that they had to show interest, every one of the attendees asked at least one question, but most of the questions were unrelated. As a result, the meeting extended continuously. However, the senior technocrat did not recognize this until she inquired and realized that her subordinates viewed the meetings a waste of their operational-time as well. Aware of the significance every individual within the organization placed on stature and being informed, she had trepidation that the unsolicited individuals would feel snubbed and ignored.

At the moment, nonetheless, she satisfied the stature needs of her subordinates in a special way. She emailed short note that read "I have asked [John Taylor, Marian Parker, and Michael Johnson] to meet with me [Tuesday at 2] in [the third-floor conference room] to discuss [next year's capital appropriation budget]. Please attend if you think that you need the information or want to participate in the discussion. However, everyone in any event will immediately receive a complete synopsis of the dialogue and of any conclusion reached, simultaneously with a request for comments."

Where originally about two dozen employees attended and stayed for the duration of the meeting, three individuals and a notetaker now get the matter over about an hour or so. None of employees feel ignored.

Majority of technocrats know all about the unfruitful and superfluous time demands, yet technocrats are frightened to reduce them. Technocrats fear erroneously severing something vital. However, this error, if made, can be promptly rectified. If a technocrat cut so severely, one often finds out very fast.

To illustrate this point, just about every newly hired high-level technocrats of complex organizations usually initially inundate themselves with invitations. Subsequent to this is the realization that they have other duties to perform, and the invites affect their productivity. From that point on, they usually sharply trim down their accessibility. A few weeks or months later, rumors will start spreading around of how they are losing touch with their technicians. Then they usually find the balance between being exploited without productivity and using their appearances to motivate their technicians.

In actual fact, there is too much risk that technocrats will cut back. Organizations tend to overestimate rather than underestimate technocrats' duties and responsibilities and conclude that far too many things can be done by technocrats. Even very productive technocrats still do a great many unnecessary, unproductive things.

However, the best evidence that the risk of excessive trimming is baseless is that extraordinary productivity is so often attained by seriously ailing or seriously handicapping technocrats. A perfect illustration is a confidential adviser I was told about, who was virtually a dying man for whom every step was a struggle; he could only work a few hours every other day. His condition forced him to trim out everything but truly vital issues. He did not lose productivity thereby; on the contrary, he became very productive, and he went on and accomplished more than anyone else in the organization. A former prime minister described such an individual as "Lord Heart of the Matter."

This is a rare case, of course; however, it points out how much control an individual can exercise over his or her operational-time if he or she really tries and how much of the operational-time–squanderers technocrats can cutout without loss of productivity.

CHAPTER 7

Perspectives on Limiting Unproductive Functions

The subsequent three analyses address the inefficient and time-squandering behaviors over which technocrats have some control. Every technocrat should observe. Organizational technocrats, nonetheless, need to be uniformly troubled with loss of operational-time as a result of poor operations and deficient organization. Poor organizations waste every technocrat's operational-time; however, above all, it wastes their own.

Technocrats' initial task is to recognize the behaviors that waste operational-time, which usually originate from deficient operational structure and forethought. The signal that technocrats should to look for is recurring emergencies. Thus, an emergency that keeps reappearing is one that must be addressed. The annual audit emergency belongs here. Technocrats can address this man-made emergencies heroically and at a lesser expense than they could in the past with the emergence of computers.

A repeated emergency should always be anticipated. It can either be averted or decreased to a practice which technocrats can manage. The definition of practice is that it familiarized technocrats with unfamiliar operations and provides them with the skill and judgment capable of performing the task. Hence, the practice organized methodically or step by step usually enhances technocrats' knowledge and assists them in addressing similar emergencies in the future.

Repeated emergencies are not confined to private organizations only. Every year, public organizations run into one of these emergencies around the end of September and the start of November. Equally, in a highly seasonal operation, where the last quarter usually is the year's low, fourth-quarter sales and profits are unpredictable. Organizations make annual earnings predictions when they usually issue their provisional report at the end of the second quarter. Subsequent to these, during the fourth quarter, private organizations usually experience an incredible dash and organization-wide emergency action to uphold leadership and management forecast. Often, between three to five weeks, no one in leadership usually performs much work. It sometimes takes only a single stroke of the pen to solve these disasters; instead of predicting a definite year-end figure, however, forecasters and leaders now predict outcomes within range. This change now appease leaders, stockholders, and the financial community because what used to be an emergency in the past is no longer noticed within organizations, and yet the fourth quarter outcomes are now more favorable than they used to be since technocrats' operational-time is no longer being wasted on making outcomes fit forecast.

Recurring emergencies are sometimes a symptom of slovenliness and laziness. A friend of mine once told me that years ago, when he started out as a consultant, he had to learn how to tell a well-managed organization from a poorly managed one, without any pretense to production knowledge. As soon as he learned, he quickly realized that a well-managed organization is quiet. He said that an organization that is noisy, in which the epic of the organization is unfolding in front of visitors, is a badly managed organization. According to him, a well-managed organization is unexciting because emergencies are predictable and are usually transformed into habits.

Equally, he said that a well-managed governmental organization is boring. This is because the theatrical things in such organizations are fundamental decisions that make the future rather than heroics in cleaning up past concerns.

Overhiring can contribute to operational-time wasting. Sometimes organizations experience undeniably too little manpower for its organizational tasks; in that case, organizations' work suffers. However, this is not the norm. What is common within organizations is a labor force that is too large for operational productivity, a labor force that often spends an ever-increasing amount of operational-time interacting with each other than working.

There are reasonable dependable indicators of overhiring. If technocrats spend more than a tiny proportion of their operational-time on issues of human relations, on arguments and misunderstandings, on jurisdictional disagreements, and questions of teamwork, then the labor force is certainly too large. In this environment, technocrats usually get into each other's territory, impeding each other's performance rather than enhancing it. In slimmed-down organizations, technocrats have room to move without interfering with each other and can do their job devoid of explaining it every time.

The justification usually given for overhiring is that there has to be an extra body to assist with work. Certain individuals are not being used effectively or at all; however, organizations need them around in case they need someone to perform specific tasks, and they have to be familiar with the organization's problems and also be a part of the team from the start. Organizations usually only have teams that comprise only of certain specializations that are needed to perform various tasks. Organizations often enlist technocrats with expertise that they usually need intermittently for specialized guidance. In some circumstances, it is considerably cost-effective to hire a consultant and consult with them for a fee than to have them in the group within organizations doing nothing productive; underhired but overskilled individuals that have the productivity of an entire group can only contribute mischief.

One more operational-time–wasting factor is deficient organization. Its indicator is excessive meetings. A meeting by description is a compromise to lacking organizations. Technocrats meet or work; they cannot do both at the same time. In an ideal world, there would be no meetings. Technocrats would know what they need to know to perform their task. Every technocrat would have the resources available to them to perform their duties. Meetings are usually held because technocrats perform different tasks and have to cooperate to get specific tasks done. Technocrats meet because the expertise and experience needed in a particular situation are not available in a single technocrat's head but have to be brought together out of the experience and skill of several technocrats.

There will forever be too many meetings. Technocrats will always demand so much teamwork that the efforts of well-meaning technocrats to create opportunities for collaboration may be rather unnecessary. However, technocrats in organizations spend more than a fairly minuscule part of their operational-time in meetings; it is a sign of deficient organization.

Each meeting engenders a multitude of small follow-up meetings. Some meetings are official, some unofficial; nonetheless, both usually go on for hours at a time. Meetings, consequently, need to be decisively controlled. An uncontrolled meeting is not just an annoyance; it is also a danger to organizations' productivity. Above all, meetings have to be the exception rather than the rule. Organizations in which technocrats meet all the time are usually unproductive organizations in which no one gets things done. Whenever an operational-time log shows the oily disintegration of meetings and whenever, for instance, technocrats in most organizations find themselves in meetings 25 percent of the time or more, there is operational-time–squandering deficient organization.

There are exemptions to this, particularly organizations such as the Security and Exchange Commission whose responsibility is protect investors; maintain fair, orderly, and efficient markets; and facilitate capital formation. However, as some of these organizations realized a while ago, individuals who sit on the board cannot be permitted to do nothing, for the same reason judges are not permitted to be advocates during their extra time.

As a policy, meetings should never be permitted to develop into the most important requirement on technocrats' operational-time. Numerous meetings usually signify deficient and erroneous organizational functions and mechanisms. They indicate that tasks that should be within a single task order or in a single component are distributed over numerous mechanisms. They also indicate that accountability is dispersed and that information is not addressed to technocrats who need to know.

Prior to 1900, the main cause of an outbreak of meetings within complex organizations was due to conventional but antiquated organizational operations. Subsequent to 1900, the U.S. government required that all departments and divisions be led directly by specific departmental or divisional leaders. However, most of these organizations were separate, each with their own clients. They were sometimes alternatives, as well as complements, to each other. Each of these organizations were expected to be the most economical and most advantageous in their service areas under certain conditions. In this sense, they were competitors. Notwithstanding, merging these organizations often yielded increased performance capabilities, which no single organization yielded by itself.

The missing piece within these organizations was clear policies. These organizations needed a clear perspective of whether to press on with all aspects of operations, in competition with each other, whether to make one the foremost operation and consider the other a complement. They needed direction on how to divide available resources among the operations. Above all, these organizations should have articulated the reality of their operations, providing the same service for the same customer base. Instead, the operations were divided among the departments, each protected from the other by layers of department, and each with its own rituals and with no assurance that each will enjoy 75 percent of the operations over the years.

Consequently, the departments were engaged in persistent meetings for years. Since each reported to a different individual within the organization, these meetings attracted administrative leaders and technocrats. Finally, the operations were cut loose from their original departments and consolidated into a single organization under one leadership. There was still a good deal of infighting going on, and big strategic decisions were unaddressed. Nonetheless, they had established some underlined understanding as to some of the major decisions. The consolidation of the organization stopped the turf wars among the leaders and subsequently brought down the total meeting time to a fraction of what it used to be.

The last vital factor of operational-time wasting is information breakdown. Technocrats in complex organizations were plagued for years by phone calls from other employees asking for vital information. These technocrats knew that they were not privy to some of the information requested of them, yet they invariably offer some form of information. The individuals that were privy to the information were not immediately asked at the time the information was really needed. The supervisors privy to the needed information usually failed to disseminate the information. It did not take a genius to correct this; at the time, all that was needed was an extra carbon chit that goes from one department leader to another who is responsible for a specific operation.

Worse, but common, is information in the wrong form. Complex organizations typically suffer from operation figures that have to be translated before operating technocrats can use them. They report averages; that is, the averages some technocrats need to function. Other technocrats usually did not need the averages but the range and the limits, service operation, and operation variations, duration of operation, and so on. To get what they need, they usually spend hours each day adapting the averages or building their own secret operations. Operational advisers usually had all the information, no one at the time usually thought about addressing the problem.

Some time-consuming operational deficiencies such as overhiring, deficient operations, or deficient information can now be corrected quickly. In the past, it took time and meticulous work to right these. The outcomes of such work were immense, particularly in terms of operational-time achieved.

Perspectives on Merging Technocrats Optional Operational-Time: Technocrats who log and evaluate their operational-time and then endeavor to control it will usually be able to decide how much operational-time they have for vital tasks. How much optional operational-time they have to accomplish major tasks can actually make a difference. The optional time technocrats usually have is often inconsequential to make any difference regardless of how ruthless they manage their operational-time.

One of the most accomplished time-conscious individuals I have ever met was a senior military officer in the U.S. Army with whom I had meetings twice a week. My meetings with him were always about an hour long. The officer was always prepared for the meeting, and soon I learned to do my homework, too. There was never more than one item on the agenda. However, when I had been in his office for about thirty minutes, he will turn around and say, "Dauphin, I believe you'd better sum up now and outline what we should do next." And about an hour after I had entered his office, he is at the door shaking my hand and saying goodbye.

After this had gone on for about a year, I finally asked, "Why always an hour?" He answered, "That's simple. I have realized that my concentration span is about an hour. If I work on any one subject longer, I will begin to reiterate what I have been saying. Simultaneously, I have realized that nothing of significance can really be addressed in much less time. An individual does not get to the point where the individual understands what he or she talking about."

During the hour I was in his office, I never observed any incoming telephone calls, and no individual ever stuck their head to announce that someone wanted him urgently. Another thing I observed was that if he had more pressing issues to attend to around the same time, he would rather cancel the meeting than hold a rush meeting. When I asked him about the telephone calls, he said, "The individuals around here have strict orders not to interrupt my meetings except when the brigade sergeant major, battalion commander, the brigade commander, the garrison commander, the assistant commanding general, the commanding general or my wife calls." He said the battalion commander knows his schedule, the brigade sergeant major rarely calls, and the rest never called him directly. Everything else the individuals working in his office held until his meetings were completed. He said he will then use an hour to return every call and to acknowledge every message. He told me he had yet to experience a major emergency that could not wait sixty minutes. Needless to say, he accomplished more every hour than many of his colleagues that I knew get done in a week.

However, even this disciplined individual had to resign himself to having at least half his time taken up by things of trivial importance and uncertain value, things that nevertheless had to be completed: acknowledging workers and colleagues who dropped in unannounced, attending meetings which could just have proceeded without him, and deciding on daily problems that should not have reached him but consistently did.

Whenever technocrats assert that more than half of their operational-time is under their control and can accumulate and that they can spend their optional time at their discretion, I am usually certain that they have no idea where their optional time goes. Technocrats rarely have much as one quarter of their optional time actually at their disposal and available for important matters that can contribute to matters they are being paid to perform. This is a fact in any complex organization except those where the unproductive optional-time demands on technocrats tend to be even higher than the productive time demands.

The greater the responsibility of technocrats, usually the more time under their control, but usually, the more time they have often makes any significant difference. The more complex the organization, the more time technocrats need to keep operations together and the implementation process moving than to make it functional and productive.

Most technocrats therefore know that they have to merge their optional time. They know that they need large portions of operational-time and that small portions are no time at all. Even if a quarter of technocrats' working days are merged in large operational-time units, it is usually not enough to get any significant job done. Even three quarters of their working days will prove useless if in a day they are only available fifteen minutes here or half an hour there.

The final step in relation to optional time involves the merging of the optional time that time logs and evaluation show and that technocrats usually obtain and control. There are so many ways of doing this: some technocrats, especially experienced ones, work at home one day a week; this is a particularly common method of merging optional time and operational-time. Others schedule all operating work, meetings, assessments, and more three days a week—for instance, Monday, Wednesday, and Friday—and set aside the mornings of the remaining days for constant, ongoing work on key issues.

However, the method by which technocrats will merge their time is far less significant than the approach. Most technocrats embark upon their work by combining the less important and less productive matters together, thus creating space between them. This technique does not usually prove productive; nevertheless, some technocrats give priority to less significant endeavors, meaning that they prioritize the things that have to be done even though they contribute little to organizations' productivity.

Consequently, every new time demand on technocrats is usually satisfied at the expense of the optional time and of the job they should perform. Consequently, some of the optional time that technocrats usually accumulate are sometimes squandered by addressing new emergencies, urgencies, and details.

Thus, technocrats should start out by assessing how much optional time they can practically have. Then they should set aside a realistic amount of uninterrupted time if they realize later that other issues will be infringing on their reserved time. They should regularly inspect their schedules to revise or eliminate unnecessary demands from fully productive activities. The understanding and perception within organizational settings is that technocrats rarely overadjust or sever unproductive times.

Technocrats should control their operational-time perpetually. Most of the time, they should not only maintain an uninterrupted schedule and evaluate it periodically; they should also set deadlines for significant activities, based on their judgment of their optional time.

A technocrat I know keeps two such lists, one for pressing matters and another for objectionable matters that have to be done, each with deadlines. When he realizes that his deadline is slipping, he knows that he is losing his time.

Time is the scarcest resource to technocrats, and unless they control it studiously, nothing whatsoever can be controlled properly. The breakdown of technocrats' time should be easily accessible and is often the method mostly used to breakdown technocratic work and to contemplate on the organizational activities that matter most.

Technocrats should know who they are—this is an old adage that sometimes eludes most human beings. However, every technocrat can follow the maxim to know their strengths if they are to be productive and successful in their endeavors.

Chapter 8

Technocratic Challenge

Technocrats can discipline themselves to function productively by using five productive technocratic steps to get astonishing things done within their organizations. Technocrats must be specialized and competent, motivated to perform productively, promote innovative ideas, enable organizations to act, and reassure organizations of productivity.

Specialized or Competent: In order for technocrats to be productive, they must be able to function competently. Technocrats must be unambiguous about their core specialization; they must operate transparently for everyone to understand their capabilities and competence. They must function from their knowledge base, operate from their competency, believe in their knowledge, and be able to defend those operational beliefs.

Persuasive qualifications of individuals' specialized knowledge on paper alone are not enough; technocrats' actions are more significant than their qualifications on paper or what they say. Technocrats' qualifications on paper and their actions must be consistent. Technocrats must prove their competence through their performance; proven accomplishment and productivity show that technocrats are extremely qualified and competent to perform their tasks. Thus, competence and specialized knowledge are fundamental to technocrats earning respect as professionals, as individuals usually assess accomplishments looking at technocrats and their qualifications.

Motivation to Perform Productively: Technocrats must be motivated to perform their jobs productively. They must assess their strengths, weaknesses, opportunities, and threats both to themselves and their organizations. They must be able to limit their organizations' weaknesses and threats and enhance their organizations' strengths and opportunities. Technocrats' understanding of organizations' operations and processes and how those could impact their organizations' future usually catapult them forward; however, an understanding of organizations' operations and processes alone is inadequate to ensure any significant productivity within an organization. Technocrats who lack organization skills will not be productive because they can only utilize organizations' resources effectively and efficiently if they do it in an organized manner. Specialized knowledge and competence do not bring about productivity.

In order to be productive, technocrats must be knowledgeable of their organizations' operations and processes. Organizations must be convinced that technocrats are knowledgeable of their operations and processes and are capable of being productive. Technocratic work is about actions, bringing organizational resources together, and it is not a monologue. Technocrats must have intimate knowledge of an organizations' operational dreams, hopes, aspirations, visions, and values.

Technocrats infuse life into organizations' hopes and dreams and enable them to realize the exhilarating potentials that the future holds for them and their organizations. Technocrats must establish a unity-of-operations purpose by revealing to organizations how they intend effectively and efficiently manage organizations' resources and ignite the flame of productivity through competence and production. Technocrats must not be everywhere because they need to be focused on production and productivity.

Promote Innovative Ideas: Technocrats must be pioneers who are enthusiastic to step out into the unfamiliar to search for opportunities to innovate, grow, and improve. Technocrats must not be the only innovators within organizations because innovation usually emerges from the purpose and direction that leaders create.

Technocrats' fundamental contribution is usually accomplishing the goals and objectives of organizations and to be open to the challenges of implementing organizations' ideas. Technocrats are innovators within organizations.

Technocrats understand that innovation and change involve experimentation, risk, and failure. They understand that possible risks and failures of experimentation are to approach change through incremental steps and small wins. They know that the aggregate of little wins establish confidence that commitment to challenging issues is achievable and vital to long-term productivity. Technocrats are not comfortable with uncertainty and failure, which is why they usually focus their attention on the capacity of their organizations to control the risks and failures with their operations and become productive. Technocrats encourage risk-taking in order to bring about innovation.

It is outrageous to declare that technocrats who are continuously productive will eventually become unproductive and that productivity is not a process of knowledge and hard work. Technocrats learn from doing, and they learn best by performing in the face of unproductivity.

Enable Organizations to Act: Enabling organizations to act foster cooperation and bring about productivity, and that aspect of cooperation goes further than sending acquisitions via chain of command. Organizations must involve technocrats who are the implementers of organizations' tasks and also individuals who will have to live with the outcome. Within current "virtual" organizations, operational planning cannot be limited to leaders and select individuals; organizational technocrats must also be involved in organizations' operational planning process as they are the converters of organizations' visions and dreams.

Organizations must make it possible for technocrats to perform outstandingly. Technocrats who are expected to accomplish outcomes must feel a sense of personal control in and rights to the process. Organizations must understand that the usual command-and-control mechanism no longer works in current work environments; instead, organizations must work to ensure that technocrats feel that they are supported, encouraged, and given the free hand to innovate. Organizations must enable technocrats to act by empowering them and not by consolidating power; hence, organizations must strengthen technocrats' capability to make good on their specialization and competence.

Organizations' ability to enable technocrats to act is essential because sometimes organizations neither give technocrats the ability to perform at their capability nor provide them the necessary resources, which usually result in inadequate resources and unproductivity. Organizations must enable technocrats to perform capably as organizations and technocrats' relationships are based on the trust and confidence that organizations will provide technocrats with the resources to perform, and technocrats will perform productively and to expectation. Through this relationship, technocrats are able to transform organizations' goals and objectives to productivity.

Reassure Organizations of Productivity: Productivity is a grueling and lengthy process. Organizations' resources sometimes get drained and depleted, and in some cases, organizations' leaders get exasperated by the rate of progress and want to give up. This is the time technocrats must reassure organizations of potential productivity. Technocrats' unpretentious acts of encouragement usually elevate the spirit and draw organizations forward, and sometimes, these encouragements come in the form of small consistent productivity.

A part of technocrats' responsibility is to ensure that organizations are aware of their contributions and to establish an environment for productivity. These are not about fun and games, even though technocrats must create an environment that is conducive to the free flow of operational information to reassure organizations of productivity. Encouragement and the assurance of productivity are not about pretentious acts designed to create some phony sense of confidence.

When organizations observe technocrats giving boisterous assurances, they repel in disgust. Encouraging organizations is a serious matter as it is how technocrats can visualize and invest their resources to enhance productivity from mishap, establish innovative programs, or make a major change of any kind. Technocrats must ensure that organizations are aware of the benefit that their actions will bring. Technocrats must be aware that when organizations are authentically encouraged and reassured, they establish a strong sense of shared responsibility and communal spirit that can carry organizations through astonishingly rough periods.

In conjunction with the five productive technocratic steps, technocrats must endeavor to observe these ten characteristics for productivity:

1. Appropriate specialization and competency to perform organizations' tasks
2. Proper identification of operational tasks
3. Establishing operational parameters by aligning technocrats' actions with organizations' goals and objectives
4. Planning for productivity by thinking constructively of organizations' operations and processes
5. Promoting innovative ideas
6. Collaborating with organizations to promote productivity
7. Understanding that with innovation comes risk—and sometimes failure
8. Knowing that small consistent productive work leads to larger ones
9. Promoting productive operational functions
10. Celebrating organizations' productivity by being more productive

Chapter 9

Perspectives on Technocratic Qualities and Characteristics

Productive technocrats must possess both talent and skill. Technocratic specializations can be acquired through training, mentoring, and experience. If technocrats are void of natural talent, the possibility of success diminishes significantly. Hence, some organizations are usually more proactive than others in identifying and developing productive technocrats. There are six common productive technocratic traits: persuasion, collaboration, realism, contributive relationship, developing worth, enhancement of products and services, flexibility, methodical approach, troubleshooting skills, and facilitative qualities.

Persuasion: Technocrats with effective persuasion skills are able to convince organizations of the importance of proceeding with or terminating certain projects that they think are important or unnecessary. Technocrats with effective persuasion skills are usually able to process information and then transmit them clearly to organizations' governance teams. They are usually able to understand, decipher, and relate their ideas to their projects and their organizations effectively.

Equally, technocrats without effective persuasion skills usually mistake communication for persuasion, and this usually leads to ineffective persuasion, leaving technocrats unable to identify the seriousness of their problem.

Some organizations' operational failure can be attributed to ineffective persuasion. Ineffective persuasive skills usually create misconceptions about the state of operations, impractical expectations, misunderstanding of goals and finance, and suspicion. A well-thought-out persuasive strategy usually helps prevent such concerns.

Effective persuasion is different from effective communication. Persuasion is about making another person accept their perspective, which involves trusting the person's knowledge, skills, and abilities, whereas effective communication involves speaking clearly and convincingly regardless of a person's knowledge, skills, or abilities.

Collaborative Trait: Being collaborative is a vital characteristic that most technocrats possess. Technocrats who are productive are able to collaborate with individuals in governance positions to promote and implement organizations' goals and objectives and thereby create positive outcomes.

Realism: Technocrats have to stay in the present for them to work productively. They cannot afford to be unrealistic because in most cases, their specialization cannot allow them to pursue unrealistic goals. Realism enables them to assist organizations with their goals, objectives, and their operational plans. It also enables technocrats to view organizations' operations concretely instead of abstractly and identify workable solutions for potential concerns.

Contributive Relationship: Technocrats' professional relationships with individuals in governance in organizations are contributive in nature. Technocrats create relationships that can help organizations achieve their goals and objectives. These relationships do not have to be of a personal nature, but they have to be professional relationships built on trust on technocrats' knowledge, expertise, ideas, and suggestions on how their organizations can operate productively.

Developing Worth: Technocrats' specialization coupled with their knowledge, experience, and talents produces productivity and cultivates and increases the worth of organizations. Worth cultivation does not only mean the increase in the financial worth of organizations; it may also be the worth of certain social service programs to citizens. The creation of organizations' worth is at the heart of technocrats' responsibility.

Enhancement of Products/Services: Technocratic work involves the enhancement of organizations' products and services. Product and service enhancement in this case is different from development. Enhancement means improving the features of already existing products and services. Technocratic work within organizations is mostly the enhancement of products and services unless they are working in organizations involved in the research and development of such products and services.

Flexibility: Technocrats are usually flexible operationally. They understand that the enhancement of products and services involve some level of disruption in the product or service because some organizations' operations are also differentiated, and there exists the possibility that the differences will be unnoticed. With disruption and differentiation comes product or service enhancement, which usually involves cost overruns, slips in schedule, and other operational emergencies. Technocrats must be flexible to constructively address the situation at hand.

Methodical Approach: Technocrats sometimes perform several operational tasks at one time. It is essential for them to first have an organized mind and understand the processes and the standard operating procedures of the various tasks that they are performing. Regardless of the technocratic work, they have to perform systematically to be productive. They have to perform methodically, reviewing schematics, books, logs, registers, and more.

Troubleshooting Skills: Technocrats have diagnostic or investigative skills. Technocratic work involves identifying the right solution to problems or concerns and requires that technocrats understand the various dynamics of tasks and ways to tactically, technically, and proficiently address issues and concerns when and if they arise.

Facilitative Quality: Technocrats have facilitative qualities in that they are able to instruct, teach, and persuade others to understand the operational significance of a task, or lack thereof. Technocrats usually work within teams regardless of the technocratic work, be it production, services, or in academia. They work in sections, squads, or, in the case of academia, departments. This team aspect requires them to be able to facilitate and instruct their colleagues or inexperienced technocrats.

Microtechnocratic Traits

There are certain traits that technocrats possess that enable them to enhance their operational interactions within organizations. These traits fall into four categories: personal, operational, persuasive, and collaborative. Personal traits involve intrinsic motivation, integrity, dependability, knowledgeability, self-assurance, studiousness, and adaptability. Operational traits involve organization/industry knowledge, knowing when to innovate, organization, basic project management skills, and operational hierarchy. Persuasive traits involve written persuasion, public speaking, constructive feedback, active listening, specificity, and organizing presentations. Collaborative traits involve operational focus, intermediary skills, consensus building, being detailed, cooperation, and value to organizations.

Personal Traits

Intrinsic Motivation: Technocrats are intrinsically motivated; they usually lack the skill and patience to motivate others. They can be accurately described as intellectuals who focus on operational processes and procedures and less on inspiring others to work. They perform well when they independently function or work directly with other technocrats who are not of equivalent experience and knowledge but have the capacity to learn and operate at the same level.

Integrity: Organizations trust competent and hardworking technocrats. Integrity comes with the competence to perform or accomplish what technocrats say they can do, and they do them enthusiastically. Organizations value them not only because of their technocratic skills but also because of the value they bring to organizations.

Dependability: Technocrats must be dependable and reliable. Organizations must trust their expertise, knowledge, and their suggestions. Organizations' survival is mostly dependent on technocratic works and suggestions.

Knowledgeability: Technocrats must be knowledgeable of their specialization and work. Operational tasks are what technocrats of varying specializations perform within organizations. Technocratic knowledge creates productivity and enhances the worth of organizations. Being hopeful does not create productivity and worth; actual efficient and effective performance does.

Self-Assurance: Technocrats must be self-assured of their abilities and their abilities to perform organizations' tasks. It fosters innovation and productivity within organizations. Conversely, lack of self-assurance produces unproductivity as it fosters indecision in their technocratic abilities and their abilities to perform productively.

Studiousness: Technocrats are studious enough to learn and update themselves on their specializations and to learn, update, and improve organizations' operational processes and procedures.

Adaptability: Technocrats easily adapt with organizations' operational changes, as long as these do not counter technocratic specialization. They are usually able to adjust, update, and enhance organizational processes.

Operational Traits

Technocrats of every specialization must possess some level of their organizations' administrative operational acumen. Technocrats need not involve themselves in governance to be familiar with their organizations' fundamental operational principles and practices. This helps technocrats identify the strengths, weaknesses, opportunities, and threats to their organizations.

Organization/Industry Knowledge: Technocrats must understand the basic processes and procedures not only of their organizations but also of other organizations involved in similar operational processes. This organization and industry knowledge enhances technocrats' experience, knowledge, and skill, thereby positioning them to provide valuable, up-to-date work and advice to their organizations.

Knowing When to Innovate: Technocrats must know when to engage in innovation and must be capable of identifying products and services that need innovation or improvement. Also, they must be confident that their proposed innovation or improvement will enhance their organizations' operational processes.

Organization: Organization is a vital component of technocratic work. Technocrats must be able to keep track of operational projects and the various resources, i.e., equipment, tools, and personnel, with the purpose of monitoring the various stages of their operations in order to be productive.

Basic Project Management Skills: Technocrats possess basic project management skills. These skills enable them to manage their and other technocrats' work to ensure that they are all on the same page. It also involves the management of other resources that pertain to their work.

Operational Hierarchy: Technocrats must understand their organizations' operational hierarchy both technically and administratively. Understanding organizations' operational hierarchy will not only help them technically; it will also help them maneuver tactically within their organizations to get things done. An understanding of organizations' operational hierarchy assists technocrats with the politics within their organizations. It helps them understand organizations' administrative rules and regulations that involve confidentiality, harassment, proper recruiting, selection, hiring, and termination practices.

Persuasive Traits

Technocrats must be persuasive to be effective and productive. These involve written persuasion, public speaking, constructive feedback, active listening, specificity, and presentation of ideas.

Written Persuasion: Technocrats must know how to write technically, proficiently, and persuasively in order to transmit their ideas correctly. *Technically*, *proficiently*, and *persuasively* because technocratic writing not only involves grammatically correct writing but also involves being technically correct based on the ethos of specialization.

Public Speaking: Technocratic public speaking involves understanding the basics of conventional public speaking rules, i.e., annunciating your words and concise communication of ideas. It also involves technocrats' understanding of the tactical and technical jargons of the specialization to accurately explain their ideas.

Constructive Feedback: Technocrats must understand how to respond to organizations' inquiries in a manner that is tactically and technically correct and to persuade inquirers of their knowledge and expertise of a given question or topic.

Active Listening: Technocrats must acquire the vital persuasive skill of listening and ensure that they understand what is being said to or asked of them. Actively listening enables technocrats to respond accurately to the questions or comments on the floor. It also portrays a notion of trying to understand someone else's perspective prior to responding to their questions or comments.

Specificity: Technocrats must be specific when requesting or inquiring about operational processes, procedures, or acquisitions. Specificity ensures that ambiguities are eliminated from whatever requests or inquiries being made.

Presentation of Ideas: Technocrats must know how to present their ideas in a technically clear and concise manner. One way is by using PowerPoint, abbreviating the most important aspects of their presentations.

Collaborative Traits

Technocrats possess certain collaborative traits, which include operational focus, intermediary skills, consensus building, being detailed, cooperation, and value to organizations. These are the collaborative traits that technocrats must possess in order to be productive.

Operational Focus: Technocrats must focus on every aspect of their organizations' operations and not only on those that are part of their scope. Focusing on organizations operationally enables technocrats to impartially and holistically provide organizations with tactical and technical professional advice.

Intermediary skills: Technocrats serve as intermediaries between organizations and productivity. The products or services that technocrats produce usually decide the productivity—or lack thereof—of organizations.

Consensus Building: Technocrats are consensus builders in that they establish agreement between organizations' goals and objectives and the executions on such. Organizations usually become productive when technocrats efficiently and effectively own their end of their agreements.

Being Detailed: Due to the nature of technocratic work, technocrats have to be detailed if they are to be productive. Technocratic specializations are usually based on standard operating procedures that, even though not binding, are fundamental to the specialization.

Cooperation: Technocrats must cooperate with organizations by informing them of operational updates in their various specializations and updating them on positive and not-so-positive operational processes.

Value to Organizations: Technocrats are valuable to their organizations in that they are the producers of organizations' productivity and worth. Absent technocratic work, organizations will be left with a bunch of ideas that cannot be implemented or followed through by anyone.

Chapter 10

Operational Differences between Technocratic Work and Governing

Enhancing Worth vs. Enhancing Motivation: Technocrats are the only individuals within organizations that enhance organizations' worth by being productive, and they sometimes even decrease worth by engaging in unproductive activities that can undermine the worth of organizations' products or services. Conversely, individuals in governance positions enhance motivation by creating environments that motivate others to perform exceptionally, i.e., by providing economic rewards, by leading considerately, and by their own actions.

Circles of Success vs. Circles of Authority: By the nature of technocrats' specializations, they are responsible for the operational success of organizations, and individuals in governance are responsible for providing operational resources, i.e., workers, equipment, products, etc., and for creating an environment conducive to productive work.

Operational Responsibility vs. Administrative Responsibility: Technocrats ensure that the operations of organizations' processes are successful whereas individuals in governance ensure that organizations function the way they are intended to, i.e., attendance, salaries, and more.

Thus, *technocratic work* and *governance* are not synonymous. It is not supposed to be common occurrence for technocrats to assume governing roles; the two roles are really distinct in function and in the manner they contribute to the accomplishment of organizations. An understanding of the difference between technocratic work and governing will enable individuals within organizations to function effectively.

A new perspective is required in order to comprehend the dissimilarity between technocratic work and governance, and to establish the path, organizations need specializations, and thereby the individuals with operational knowledge, to function productively. Technocrats are responsible for operational processes and ensure that workers, machinery, and tools operate efficiently. They ensure that organizations hire workers who are knowledgeable and well trained and that organizations acquire capable and optimal tools, machineries, and equipment. Conversely, individuals in governance ensure that employees have confidence in their organizations' administrative and operational processes and sustainability.

Individuals in governance must have a clear understanding of their organizations' necessary operations. Individuals in governance positions are usually responsible for the hiring process, and it is vital that they understand the differences between technocratic work and governing. Governing is about creating purpose, direction, and motivation; technocratic work is about specialization and a clear understanding of operational processes.

Workers within organizations must understand the difference between technocratic work and governance if they have any intention of advancing within their organizations. Even if they are only assuming these positions temporarily, they need to understand the differences to perform effectively. Individuals mostly learn from doing; nonetheless, every individual can only perfect what emerges naturally, be it technocratic traits or governance traits.

Technocrats have colleagues and mentees by virtue of their specializations, experience, knowledge, and longevity; organizations give some technocrats accountability and responsibilities for their teams, sections, or functions. In most cases, titles are inconsequential, and they are usually ceremonial in nature.

Technocrats are usually not in positions of authority unless when asked to assume one. However, technocratic work is transactional, and technocrats work directly and collaboratively with individuals in governance positions to ensure that organizations' operations and processes are tended to effectively and productively.

Technocrats are paid to perform operational tasks that include service or manufacturing, usually within the confines of time and money, and the restriction and focus are usually operational rather than administrative.

Technocrats tend to be meticulous and focused; they usually prefer stability and calm. They are usually relatively risk-averse, they usually try to elude conflict as much as possible, and they generally prefer operating in stable and calm environments. Technocrats usually avoid risks because of the nature of their responsibilities: they simply cannot afford to take them. Technocrats are individuals who usually proceed systematically and methodically as their specialization skills require.

Conversely, individuals in governance positions are usually risk takers and charismatic. Being charismatic does not mean that these individuals have flamboyant personalities. It means that they usually have good people skills and possess an unassuming style that gives credit to individuals who deserve it and accept blame when it is warranted. This usually enables them to be effective at establishing loyalty and productivity.

The description of risk takers implies that they are risk seekers, which is inaccurate because they are not blind thrill seekers. They are comfortable taking risk if they perceive it as a natural process to avert or overcome problems and to get things done.

Research findings have shown that a surprising number of individuals in governance positions have had some form of handicap that they have had to overcome, i.e., traumatic childhoods, dyslexia, shorter-than-average height, and these handicaps have probably taught them to have an independent mind that is required to stretch limits and not be bothered about what others think about them.

The Big Picture

There are certain salient distinctive differences between technocrats and governance. These vital differences are in terms of attributes.

Technocrats have the ability to facilitate, accept the status quo, and are pragmatic in accepting trends and events but go no further. Their focus is on control, structure, and systems. They have a linear perspective, only following what is at the end of their noses and asking a limited set of questions—how or when? They imitate other technocrats, perceive operational threats, and minimize operational weaknesses.

Governance is about studying and developing ideas and principles and being innovative and resourceful and looking for solutions to problems. Governance is empathetic, with a focus on workers, inspires trust among stakeholders, understands the big picture, requires superior listening skills, courageously challenges the state of affairs, and asks why and what can be improved. It looks for opportunities to develop strengths, and it also develops managers.

These individuals in governance are the causal force that initiates things that will otherwise not occur without their interference. They are futuristic individuals that envision possibilities that are usually synonymous with the past. They are skillful at motivating workers, communicating their vision clearly, serving as architects of organizations' strategies, and inspiring growth and improvement of workers on behalf of their visions. They are usually rich in strength of character and are resolute.

Technocrats oversee operational quality, and at their peak, they produce beyond expectations. They provide organizations with reliability, certainty, and predictability, all of which are essential to the viability and longevity of organizations. Technocrats are involved in continuous project enhancement, monitor progress against objectives, and track and report data that allows for solid fact-based decisions. Technocrats initiate ideas and strategies within organizations and sometimes are involved in cross-functional projects.

Individuals in governance positions are required to establish a strong communication pipeline and to promote and reward productivity, distinct skill sets, actions, behaviors, and competencies as well as take thoughtful actions to guarantee that technocrats receive the support required to produce productively.

Table 3: Differences between Leaders and Managers

Subject	Technocratic Work	Governance
Essence	Stability	Success
Focus	Operational process	Administration
Have	Operational resources	People
Horizon	Productivity	Efficiency and effectiveness
Seeks	Outcomes	Vision
Approach	Meticulous planning	Purpose and direction
Decision	Production	Decision
Power	Operational authority	Formal authority
Appeal to	Organization	Heart
Energy	Process	Procedural
Culture	Assimilation	Mold
Dynamic	Reactive	Preemptive
Persuasion	Produce	Convince
Style	Transactional	Transformational
Exchange	Productive for work	Intrinsic and extrinsic rewards
Likes	Constancy	Deeds

Wants	Accomplishments	Results
Risk	Risk-averse	Risk taking
Rules	Conformist	Creates
Conflict	Avoids	
Direction	Existing Path	New Path
Truth	Establisher	Seeker
Concern	Realistic	Abstract
Credit	Maker	Giver
Blame	Predictable	Unpredictable

REFERENCES

Adler, N. J. (2010). Going beyond the dehydrated language of management: leadership insight. *Journal of Business Strategies*, Vol. 31 (No. 4), pp. 208-221.

Benin, W. (2003). *On becoming a leader*. PA: Perseus Books Group.

Blanchard, K. & Johnson, S. (1982). One minute manager. USA: William Morrow and Co.

Collins, J. C. (2001). Good to great. HarperCollins.

Drucker, P.F. (2002). The effective executive. NY: Harper Collins.

Harland, P. (1994) Economic crisis and the centralization of control over the managerial process: Corporate restructuring and neo-Fordist decision-making. *American Sociological Review*, 59: 723-745.

Kouzes, J.M. & Posner, B.Z. (2003). Leadership the challenge. United States: Jossey-Bass

Linfield, L. (2013). The big difference between leaders and managers. The Business of HR. Retrieved from http://www.tlnt.com/2013/07/02/the-big-difference-between-leaders-and-managers/ December 20, 2013.

Nayar, V. (2013). Three differences between managers and leaders. Harvard Business Review. Retrieved from http:blogs.hbr.org/2013/08/tests-of-a-leadership-transiti/ on December 12, 2013.

PHD in Management.org (2011). 25 qualities and characteristics of a good manager. Retrieved from http://phdinmanagement.org/25-qualities-and-charateristics-of-a-good-manager.html. on December 11, 2013.

Quinn, J. B. (1992). Intelligent enterprise. New York: Free Press.

Roberts, B. C., Loveridge, R., Gennard, J. & Eason, J. V. (1972). Reluctant militants: a study of industrial technicians. London: Heinemann.

Ruzic, N. P. (1981). The automated factory. In Tom Forester (ed.), the microelectronics revolution: 165 173. Cambridge. MA: MIT Press.

Saunders, D (2006). Mastering the differences between leadership and management. Retrieved from http://www.articlesbase.com/management-articles/mastering-the-difference-between-lead... on December 20, 2013.

Scarselletta, Mario 1996 "The infamous lab error: Education, skill and quality in medical technicians' work." In Stephen R. Barley and Julian Orr (eds.). Between Craft and Science: Technical Workers in U.S. Settings. Ithaca, NY: ILR Press (forthcoming).

Scherer, F. M. & Huh, K. (1992). Top managers' education and r & d investment. *Research Policy*. 21: 507-511.

Scott, W. R. (1981). *Organizations: rational, natural and open systems*. New York: Prentice-Hail.

Shaiken, Harley 1984 Work Transformed: Automation and Labor in the Computer Age. New York: Holt, Rinehart, and Winston.

Silvestri, George, and John Lucasiewicz 1991 "Occupational employment projections." Monthly Labor Review, Winter: 64-94.

Smith, Chris 1987 Technical Workers: Class, Labour and Trade Unionism. London: MacMillan.

Spenner, Kenneth I. 1979 "Temporal changes in work content." American Sociological Review, 44: 968-975 1983 "Temporal change in the skill level of work." American Sociological Review, 48: 824-837.

Straker, D. (2012). Leadership vs. Management. Changing Minds. Retrieved from http://changingminds.org/disciplines/leadership/articles/mamager_leader December20, 2013.

Steinberg, Ronnie J. 1990 "Social construction of skill: Gender, power. and comparable worth." Work and Occupations, 17: 449-482.

Strauss, Anselm, Leonard Schatzman, Rue Bucher, Danuta Ehrlich, and Melvin Sabshin 1964 Psychiatric Ideologies and Institutions. Glencoe, IL: Free Press.

Szafran, Robert F. 1992 "Measuring occupational change over four decennial censuses: 1950-1980." Work and Occupations, 19: 293-327.

Taitro, Donna 1992 "The impact of information technology of office personnel staff at Cornell University." Working paper, Cornell Information Technologies, Cornell University.

Taylor, Frederick Winslow 1911 The Principles of Scientific Management. New York: Norton.

Thompson, James D. (1967). Organizations in Action. New York: McGraw-Hill.

U.S. Department of Labor (1977). Dictionary of Occupational Titles. Washington. DC: U.S. Government Printing Office.

Van Maanen, John, and Stephen R. Barley 1984 "Occupational communities: Culture and control in organizations." In Barry M. Staw and Larry L. Cummings (eds.), Research in Organizational Behavior. 6: 287-365. Greenwich. CT: JAI Press.

Wallace, Jean E. 1995 "Organizational and professional commitment in professional and nonprofessional organizations." Administrative Science Quarterly, 40: 228-255.

Weber, Max 1968 Economy and Society Berkeley, CA: University of California Press.

Whalley, Peter, and Stephen R. Barley 1996 "Technical work in the division of labor: Stalking the wily anomaly." In Stephen R. Barley and Julian Orr (eds.), Between Craft and Science: Technical Workers in U.S. Settings. Ithaca, NY: ILR Press (forthcoming).

Winch, Graham, and Eric Schneider 1993 "Managing the knowledge-based organization: The case of architectural practice." Journal of Management Studies. 40: 923-938.

Womack, James P., Daniel T. Jones, and Daniel Roos 1990 The Machine That Changed the World: The Story of Lean Production. Cambridge, MA: MIT Press.

Zabusky, Stacia 1996 "Computers, clients and expertise: Negotiating technical identities in a non-technical world." In Stephen R. Barley and Julian Orr (eds.), Between Craft and Science: Technical Workers in U.S. Settings. Ithaca, NY: ILR Press (forthcoming).

Zabusky, Stacia, and Stephen R. Barley 1996 "Redefining success: Ethnographic observations on the careers of technicians." In Paul Osterman (ed.). Broken Ladders: White-Collar Careers in Transition. Cambridge: Cambridge University Press (forthcoming).

Zuboff, S. (1989). *In the age of the smart machine*. New York: Basic Books.

www.ingramcontent.com/pod-product-compliance
Lightning Source LLC
Chambersburg PA
CBHW021006180526
45163CB00005B/1907